PROMOTE YOUR SPIRITUAL BUSINESS

by Vanessa Jones

Techniques and tips for marketing for the conscious entrepreneur
and business.

Vanessa Jones © 2015

Promote Your Spiritual Business

This publication is designed to provide accurate and authoritative information for marketing in business. It is sold under the express understanding that any decisions or actions you take as a result of reading this book must be based on your commercial judgement and will be at your sole risk. The author will not be held responsible for the consequences of any actions and/or decisions taken as a result of any information given or recommendations made.
Every attempt was made to ensure information was accurate at time of publication.

Contents

Introduction.. 6

Who is this book for?.................................. 8

Don't be afraid! 10

What is marketing?.................................. 11

The Lightworker-Technology Syndrome............. 13

Purification spell powder........................ 17

Marketing and spirituality: the false dichotomy.......... 19

Intention 22

The team 24

Numerology in marketing 27

Intuitive knowledge 28

What do you want?................................ 32

Branding 34

Mission statement................................ 39

Business name 42

Naming meditation 43

Identifying your target demographics........... 45

Market research 49

Social media marketing 52

    Social media policy 54

    Blogging 55

    Blog planner template....................................... 67

    Blog promotion 70

    Blogging by your star sign 76

    Enewsletter.. 79

    Facebook 91

    Twitter 103

    Instagram 112

    YouTube 115

    LinkedIn.. 120

    Google+ 122

Websites.. 123

    Your products/services 128

    Content tips 130

    Online courses 132

    Google Analytics 133

SEO 134

    Useful programs 138

Customers and sales 141

    The Pareto Principle 141

    Keeping your customers loyal...........................143

    Upselling...145

    Product promotional strategy 146

FAQ 149

Introduction

At the time of creating this book, I am working as a marketing manager for a not-for-profit arts organisation. I am lucky that I get to experiment and incorporate spiritual concepts and beliefs into my work. Combining my social media knowledge and skills with my intuition, deep inner guidance and drawing on my spiritual knowledge and concepts I have been able to increase the organisation's Facebook following by nearly 220 per cent and their Twitter followers by nearly a thousand per cent in less than two years. As you can imagine this has dramatically increased our client engagement, sales and resulted in a fifty per cent revenue increase. These results have really confirmed to me the power of social media in marketing activities.

In the past I have worked for various marketing agencies, as a publicist and copywriter, and have managed multiple projects for not –for-profit organisations. I love having many projects on the go at once, so I also consult in a marketing capacity to several businesses. I'm also a freelance writer and copywriter—that means I write a range of materials from magazines to websites to press ads to blogs. I have been published on a number of online publications, have several blogs and as a creative writer I am working on two novels, a book of short stories and a book of poetry. I have qualifications in professional writing and have studied philosophy and creative writing at university.

I'm very excited that I have discovered a way that works for me and others, where I can combine the traditional world of modern business with my new age philosophies and spiritual practises and rituals and this is why I felt driven to create this book.

Maybe you are in touch with your spiritual side, Mother Nature, Spirit and other transpersonal concepts and are following your intuition to explore the possibilities that you can find from combining your business "side" with your spiritual practises. Are you used to doing things as you feel guided and not always formally plan ahead? Do you often see things as a vague (or clear if you highly psychic) overall picture and Spirit grants you snapshots of things to come? I do too and I love living this way. I also like to use the left brain way of living for my marketing! There is space to incorporate intuitive methods into your marketing but I also believe in the power of strategy and loose rules and guidelines. I am grateful to your higher self that has connected with my higher self and lead you to read this book.

This book is an introduction into social media marketing combines a range of fundamental and practical aspects with an overlay of spiritual "hocus pocus" that will get you started in creating a thriving and sustainable business.

Who is this book for?

This book is a fundamental guide for simple promotional and marketing techniques that anyone can use to boost their business, whether they are a sole practising artist, medium sized enterprise or a national franchise. I have written it for businesses that focus more on a spiritual service, in the health and wellbeing industry or complementary therapies.

It's ideal for energy healers, Reiki practitioners, yoga/meditation teachers and studios, psychics/mediums, vegan/health bloggers, essential oil distributors, massage therapists, kinesiologists, acupuncturists, Feng Shui consultants, naturopaths, craft makers and so many more people in so many more professions.

Undoubtedly, you will still find benefit from the information I have to offer here if you feel like your business or service falls outside of these categories. Hairdressing salons, dancers, holiday resorts, florists, artists, musicians, writers—anyone creative— will also get tremendous value out of this information.

It's a perfect book for the beginner, who may be new to social media and marketing or you just needs some extra tips and advice to catapult your business to the next level of success that you are yearning for.

We can safely assume that if you are reading this, Spirit or your higher self has guided you to read this, for whatever reason. If you are already feeling the tingle of potential and excitement about your business growing, then that is confirmation that this book is for you and it will catapult you into the success that you are ready for.

There's a part of you thinking that you don't really need or want to delve into the world of online marketing, am I right? Perhaps you think you don't need it or don't have the time for it? Read this book, dabble in it and then make that decision. The great thing about online marketing is that what you put into it, you get in return. If you genuinely want your business to succeed, it is highly likely that you are already willing to give this book a go.

Marketing is a full time job; don't have any illusions! If you think that you will only be investing an hour a week into the marketing of your business and still expect miraculous results, you may need to reconsider. But you need to find a balance that will work for you and you need to be able to do your core service, without the marketing aspect taking over. This book will provide you with the fundamentals of marketing and some guidance of how you can implement things efficiently and effectively and still be able to invest your heart into your business.

Did you know? A survey conducted by Market Force in 2012, revealed that 74 per cent of people encouraged their friends to try new products via social media and a whopping 81 per cent tried things based on their friends' suggestions via social media. (US and UK based survey and respondents)

Don't be afraid!

Marketing, particularly digital/social media marketing, can be a daunting concept for some, especially when the thing you are trying to promote is you and your services. Our inner critic can bring up all sorts of insecurities and try to get us to believe that we're not worth promoting or people will discover we are a fraud. I can assure you that this is a feeling I am very familiar with. With every key stroke, my inner critic is deafening loud and on some days, I listen to it. But mostly, I just kept letting it have its rant and keep typing.

Promoting yourself won't be as scary as you think. I know it's new and expansive, beyond perhaps the mind can comprehend but for many of us, we have no problem in believing such intangible and esoteric concepts as Spirit, Heaven, ghosts and so forth and that these can be beautiful concepts. I feel that if you can believe in these concepts, then digital marketing will be easy for you!

Digital marketing is just like a scaled down version of the Universe, contained on some devices (such as a smart phone) that you can access anytime, in the way that you want to. It holds lots of answers and has the ability to reach a wide, connected group of people.

What is marketing?

Marketing is a broad term that is essentially a way of getting your message, your business or service, out into the world and connecting with clients/customers to get sales; although it's not always the case that the bottom line is sales.

In most instances—and the heart of this book will be—that you'll be focussing on relationship marketing—that means you will be speaking directly to the client/customer, rather than business to business (you may have seen this written as B2B elsewhere).

Under the marketing umbrella there are a few sub categories of marketing. I'll briefly describe them below:

Traditional marketing
This comprises of things that are part of your marketing plan that aren't in the online space. You can think of them as the various ways people promoted their businesses before the internet was a prominent feature of our daily lives.

It may include:
- hardcopy brochures, flyers, pamphlets, magazines etc
- print advertising—ads in newspapers, magazines etc
- PR (public relations) and media campaigns
- advertorial
- editorial
- media advertising—radio and TV commercials
- loyalty systems (such as loyalty cards, VIP memberships etc)
- branding, design and logos.

Digital marketing
Although I'll be discussing techniques from both traditional and digital marketing, *How to Promote Your Spiritual Business* will be mostly concerned with digital (or online) marketing Because a lot of digital marketing is free or relatively inexpensive. It also happens to be my area of expertise and passion.

Digital marketing is basically marketing that utilises technology; you may know it as internet or online marketing.

Digital marketing can comprise of:
- website
- social media (Facebook, YouTube, Instagram, Twitter, Pinterest etc)
- blog (web log)
- digital advertising
- enews (electronic newsletter)
- apps (phone applications for smart phones, tablets etc)
- webinars
- online courses and forums
- podcasts
- streaming media—audio/visual content
- ebooks

There are two systems of digital marketing: push and pull. Pull is when end users seek out the content and push is when you push the content towards the clients/customers without them seeking it out. We'll be looking at a push system, with the intention that it will gradually build its own pull system.

The Lightworker-Technology Syndrome

Do you have any of the following reoccurring symptoms?

- technology (such as computers, phones, photocopiers) never seem to really work for you
- your computer crashes without explanation repeatedly (even if it's new)
- your phone continuously leaves you frustrated
- it takes you two or three attempts to upload a picture or video to your computer
- do you lose files and documents continuously?

You might just have Lightworker-Technology Syndrome! I have witnessed this phenomenon in a lot of lightworkers and spiritual healers, so I've labelled it the Lightworker-Technology Syndrome.

My research into this peculiarity came up quite blank and I'm a bit flummoxed as to why this isn't written about more – perhaps every time someone tried to write about it, their computer would crash?

Here's what I believe is the cause of the Lightworker-Technology Syndrome:

Firstly, on a subconscious level you may be sabotaging yourself. You don't want to get too successful or too popular because it might mean you are too busy or it may be too scary or any number of reasons where we fear success. Take comfort in knowing that this fear resides in all of us, to varying degrees.

Often, we're not even aware of our self-sabotaging behaviour – conscious or subconscious. Have a firm – but loving – chat with yourself to let your inner being know that yes, success may be scary but that you're going to do this anyway, if only to give it a try. Remind your inner saboteur this, every time it tries to get attention. It's also worth noting the areas where you are self defeating in relation to your overarching goal. What are the limiting beliefs you dialogue with yourself?

Secondly, as someone who is deeply in touch with their spiritual self you will transmit a myriad of vibrational energy that is not entirely compatible with current technology. I suspect this is because lightworkers transmit energy at a higher and faster frequency, where as technology can be at a slower and denser frequency. I can't wait for the day when it catches up!

I've also heard a few respected lightworkers that I know comment on how when they spend a lot of time working with the light and helping others to create good in their lives the dark forces will naturally amp up their resistance in the form of technological sabotage. Those sneaky dark forces!

If this happens to you the first step is to bring it to your conscious awareness. It will be easier to tackle if you are aware of it.

Thirdly, you may have been cursed, perhaps in this life or you have inherited it from another life. Don't let this scare you as hexes and curses can be easily remedied.

Here's how to ascertain whether you've been cursed:
- Do things seem to go "wrong" for you a lot? For example, does your car break down, have you been robbed more than once,
- Does your back and shoulder region feel heavy and tense a lot?
- Do you have a new influx of unusual nightmares?
- Are you unusually clumsy or have you seen an increase in minor injuries (such as cuts on your fingers, bruises etc)?
- Does it feel like someone has shot an arrow into your head, back or chest?
- Do you feel like you are walking through sludge?

How to remedy the Lightworker-Technology Syndrome:

- sage/smudge your workspace, computer, iPad, smart phone and other areas and devices using good quality sage leaves, eucalyptus leaves or rosemary sprigs. See below for more details.

- spread a ring of salt (Epsom or sea salt works best) around your workspace
- make your own purification spell powder and sprinkle or burn it around your home or office
- burn peppermint and/or rosemary essential oils
- set a bunch of hydrangeas in your area, as they have excellent hex breaking properties
- make your workspace, office or study very unappealing for dark forces – surround yourself with things that encourage your light such as Himalayan salt lamps and inspirational pictures/quotes. It also helps if you keep your workspace well lit with as much natural daylight as possible, meditate in this space, reduce the amount of stress that you feel in this space by going for a walk or releasing stress out into nature whenever it arises, play uplifting music and chant daily using a Tibetan singing bowl.

I believe technology is an extension of my magic. I am grateful because without my computer and the internet, I wouldn't be able to spread my light and my words and thus live my divine purpose.

Spirit is amazing at guiding us in the direction that is right for us. And often, will place obstacles directly in our pathway to ensure we take a different route. Spirit can see all—the bigger picture— so it knows how to redirect us. However, let's assume you're like me and can sometimes too hastily blame Spirit for placing an obstacle in your way when it may not be that at all. How easy is it to say 'oh my computer does not work, therefore I'll have to take a day off?'

Three is a magical number for Spirit, so if you bear witness to a synchronicity three times it is Spirit acknowledging that it's heard you. So if your computer automatically shuts down, try again. Don't give up and say 'oh well obviously Spirit doesn't want me to continue with my social media today so I'm going to have a chai and pop on Dr Phil. As I said, Spirit can see the bigger picture, so only Spirit knows why it was important that your computer shut down. If your computer crashes three times then "Dr Phil permission" granted! Back away from the social media because Spirit is being undeniably clear here. Three times and Spirit is trying to get your attention.

Purification
You may often hear of rituals and suggestions that call for "purification". There can be a number of ways that you can purify a space, object or your own energy field. You may already work with a way that suits you best so by all means, continue to do so.

One of the most trusted forms of purifying something is using a smudge stick. Smudging is practise that has been appropriated from a Native American tradition where a bundle of herbs, tightly wound together, is lit and its smoke is used to cleanse an area or object. Most smudge sticks that you can purchase today consist of white sage, a powerful cleansing herb. Smudge sticks are readily available to buy but you can make your own if you are so inclined. I have made smudge sticks in the past using dried out Mulberry tree twigs, salvia, eucalyptus twigs and leaves, lavender and rosemary. The trick is to make sure you dry them out thoroughly; using the sun, a dehydrator or your oven and bind them as tight as possible using non-toxic cotton or string.

Salt is also a powerful purifier. Sea salt, Himalayan salt, rock salt—they are all really useful. You can spread it around the perimeter of your house (this will also keep out ants), as a border for self-protection when casting a spell or undergoing a ritual or sprinkle it where you feel appropriate. Epsom salts and bicarbonate of soda can be substituted (or a combination of all three salts mentioned above) which makes for a very powerful purifying powder. Use these three in the bath or shower to completely purify your body and aura.

Visualisation also works wonders! Call upon Archangel Michael and the Violet Flame to cleanse a space or visualise an area or your whole body filling with brilliant, white light, cleansing, cleaning and purifying.

I have made my own purification spell powder which contains a potent mix of herbs, plants and magic that I have created under the full moon. I use this powder for intense and dire situations or just if I want some peace of mind. I spread some across the front doorway of my house and office occasionally to ensure no negative energy or people cross that threshold. You can find your own protection or purification spell via a trusted source or ask Spirit to guide you in creating one.

Purification spell powder

Dried herbs:
I like to pick my own (after asking Mother Nature's permission) and dry them either using the sun or an oven. But you can buy them already dried in a packet. Play around with your own measurements as to what feels right. I have listed the measurements below if you get stuck, but I like to follow my intuition at the time of creating this spell power. The measurements are taken in to consideration once the herb has been dried.

Ingredients:
½ teaspoon oregano
2 clove buds
1 teaspoon rosemary
1 teaspoon mint
1 teaspoon Salvia/sage (I use salvia greggi, garden sage and pineapple sage)
3 leaves eucalyptus
½ lemon rind
Plus:
½ teaspoon black pepper
½ teaspoon sea or Himalayan salt

Optional extras (dried):

mulberry leaves
basil
chilli

Preparation:
1. Smudge yourself and the area where you will be creating the spell powder.
2. Surround yourself in crystals, white light and any other protection ritual/deities that you are called to do. I play music that cleanses my mind; play my Tibetan singing bowl and often burn peppermint oil whilst preparing this powder.
3. Mix all your dried quantities into a dedicated mortar and pestle and grind together.
4. Store in clear glass bottles.

Uses:
Spread the powder over your doorstep
Put it in your homemade incense
Mix it with essential oils and burn
Sprinkle it in a circle around your body or working space

Warning: because this contains chilli and pepper, be sure no to let it come into contact with your skin, eyes or nose.

'Having a low opinion of yourself is not "modesty". It's self destruction. Holding your uniqueness in high regard is not "egotism". It's a necessary precondition to happiness and success,'
Bobbe Sommer.

It can be a challenge for people who are on this planet solely for service to want to engage in marketing. For those new to marketing and promotional activities, it can look nefarious and deceptive and you might initially feel like it conflicts with your beliefs.

But I urge you to look deeper within to see whether it really does conflict with your beliefs or whether your very clever self-saboteur is at work again. This crafty saboteur is so clever that it will come to you in many ways, including using your own beliefs against you.

There is a saboteur in all of us, it might have a tiny voice or it might have a booming, deep voice that dominates your daily existence but it's there. And you're most at risk if you think it's not there because that means it's hiding in your internal blind spot. The more awareness you can bring to this saboteur part of yourself and the more light you can shine on it, and expose it for what it is, the easier it is to overcome.

Have your cake
I have a very grandiose vision for most of my clients, which means I am giving them a big metaphorical chocolate cake, when they may only want a forkful to taste. I believe that they are going to want the whole cake eventually, so I put it there in front of them to consume all in one sitting (one of the best parts of being a human!) or to take a slice or two and keep the rest for later.
More than one client has bristled at the idea of having a large chocolate cake laid out before them, especially if they have told themselves to stay away from cake because it might make them

overweight or unhealthy or whatever reason they've convinced themselves of for many years.
The cake is actually an analogy for the abundance and success that a healthy marketing plan can offer them.

Even if you are happy with a couple of safe clients per week, I suspect that there is still a part of you that is yearning for more, much more. You're helping no one, especially yourself, by playing small.

I don't want to make money; I'm here to serve, not to be greedy. Why do you believe that not having an abundance of money is not your birthright? Can you see all the ways that having an abundance of money, gleaned from doing what you love and running your own business, would be beneficial to you, your family and friends and the wider community?

Being poor doesn't necessarily make you more spiritual, healthier, happier or holier. It's the energetic or emotional attachment to it that can cause us damage.

From the yoga sutras:
Vairagya/Non-attachment: The essential companion is non-attachment (1.15), learning to let go of the many attachments, aversions, fears, and false identities that are clouding the true Self.

I don't need marketing; I believe that the right people will come to me.
This belief is common and I have seen it many times being the consumer and the marketer. If the right people will come to you, how can it hurt to convey your message to an even wider group of people? The "right" people will come to us if we let them know we exist and we affirm to Spirit that we are ready or willing.

I've heard the term "energy" bandied about a lot when it comes to poor sales, low attendance numbers or dwindling clients.
There seems to be a misconception that just 'putting the right

energy out there' will bring in the motherload. I agree and I disagree. Intention and energetics play a vital role but so does action. How often have you 'put energy out there' to get your groceries without having to go to the supermarket? Even if you get your groceries delivered, you still have to take the action to order them. Consider marketing your action step.

Check within yourself to see if you are holding this belief and if it is just another way your internal saboteur is trying to deceive you.

Marketing feels too manipulative.
Marketing can be manipulative, just like any industry or profession can be. Psychics and healers can be manipulative, therapists can be manipulative and so can personal trainers. But the majority are not.
Marketing is a form of communication, just like speaking, performing, singing and dancing can be. It is about conveying a message and reaching a wider audience. If all your messages come from your heart, are authentic and arise from your truth, how can it be manipulative?

Remember: that people are free to make up their own mind and have their own free will.

Intention

One of the most powerful ways to use marketing and the information you will learn from this book, is to direct your energy.

Sometimes, I couldn't see this book clearly before it was written. And I'd really fight with my mind to have a clearly produced picture of the steps I would take, the neat chronological order in which I wrote it, what was to come and what I had to write to get it complete. But this became a battle and when I was fifty thousand words through my draft, I was enjoying a session with my healer one day and I just felt the energy of the book, of my creation.

Immediately, I wanted to liken it to an object, something tangible that I could use as a visible talisman. But I graciously stopped myself and just enjoyed the feeling of the energy being there. The closest visual representation I can offer you is a warm pink glow, perhaps spherical, maybe not. I imagined myself hurling that energy at the book (as it stood; a pile of documents on my computer) and as it will stand when complete, in a tangible book format. It's this energy that I'm following – even upon completion—not the chapter breakdown in the left of my screen.

Take a moment to close your eyes and feel into the energy of where you want to be with your business and what it will look like. Don't worry too much about the how, you're aiming for a feeling or an energy.

Marketing with intention
Just because you're at the computer, smart phone or tablet to undertake your social media marketing, doesn't mean that it's any less a spiritual domain. Just like you would with meditation, space clearing, yoga or cleaning, set aside at least half an hour each working day to invest energy and time into your social media marketing. Just like meditation, some days you can really

look forward to it, some days you will engage in it mindlessly and some days it may feel like a burden. And just like meditation, regular, consistent practise is important.

I find it powerful to summon energy and create an intention when on social media platforms. Have you ever noticed that when you are feeling angry or sad that all the content on Facebook or Twitter seem to reflect this? Or when you are feeling inspired and in alignment that everybody else in your feed is enjoying the same exhilaration.

Take a few deep, purifying breaths before you start your social media tasks. Feel the excitement and joy welling in your heart space, perhaps rising up from the centre of the earth through your legs all the way up to your heart. Or it may be generated at the very core of your heart.

As you look at your screen, infuse it with love and feel it pouring out from you and permeating everything around you. Know that anyone who is out there in cyber world is benefiting now from the energy you send out. What is it that you want to achieve with your social media today? Do you want another fifty Facebook page likes? Do you want two new bookings? Do you want to make someone smile? Set your intention and feel gratitude that it is done. Once your tasks are complete, walk away from your screens and hand it over to the Universe to complete. The Universe gave us the internet, social media and the beautiful technology that abounds. Despite what a lot of people may believe, it really is a blessing that Spirit has provided for us. I am grateful and ecstatic that it exists.

The team

Marketing tools work at their most optimum when they are used together; they all talk to each other. Consider them a community or a family or a team that work together with one end goal in mind. The goal being a sale, new client/customer or an appointment.

Let's think of your marketing as a sports team and each marketing activity a player that will support and talk to other players to achieve the end goal.

The aim of marketing in this case is to score a goal and you need an effective team to do so. Are all your players pointed at the right goal posts or are they scoring for the other team? How easy is it to score a goal or orchestrate your team so that goals can be continuously scored?
In any team, it's imperative that the players work together, talk to one another and work collaboratively – and not as individuals. If one player is scoring all the goals, they are going to be exhausted quite quickly. If another player keeps kicking wide, and there's no team member there to funnel it into the goal square, then it is a wasted effort.

Clearly, I've just proven my complete lack of sporting knowledge but I'm confident that you understand the metaphor. All your marketing platforms should work in cohesion; your Twitter will direct people towards your Facebook page, your Facebook page will direct people to your website, your enews will point to all your social media platforms and so forth.

That doesn't mean that you have to engage in all the available platforms, it just means that you need to put together the team that works best for you.

There are two ways in which you can immediately identify that you have the right team:
  a) it feels right and
  b) you are enjoying it.

If your marketing is becoming a burden and you are not feeling that excitement of spreading your message, then focus on those marketing activities that do bring you joy. There's no point engaging in this aspect of your business if it detracts from the joy of providing your service or making and selling your products – which is the core reason why you're in your current business!

Remember: you can always outsource all or part of your marketing. Ask the Universe to send you the right person or people and once they show up trust them and their knowledge.

Picking your team
You can be strategic or experimental with your approach to choosing your marketing "team". You can choose a tool from a few different areas. Here's a formula you may like to use:

Website + 2 social media platforms + 1 traditional marketing platform = your marketing "family or team"

Another option is to take the scattergun approach and try as many tools as you can and see which work best for your service. Give them all at least a three month trial, observing their benefits, strengths and weaknesses and think about which ones you are more drawn to put time and effort into, which are more fun and provide more return on investment (investment being time and/or money) and which speak the best to the other tools.

It is absolutely imperative that you have a central place where you can direct all your tools towards. I highly recommend that that is your website—a place where you can easily store all your services, information, products, events etc and that people will know where to go. It is an automatic response that people will search for your website before connecting with you.

'89% of consumers will search for you using a search engine for purchase decisions. 62% also research on Facebook,' February 2012, <http://www.brafton.com/news/89-percent-of-consumers-use-search-engines-for-purchase-decisions>

If you don't have the time to invest in setting up a website (you can get them for free these days with a number of great online platforms) then maybe your Facebook page or physical premises is your central place but you will have much more success if your gateway is your website.

Numerology in marketing

Whilst I don't purport to be an expert numerologist, I strongly believe in and adhere to the power of numbers. Here are some ways in which you can incorporate numerology into your marketing activities.

1. Schedule or post your social media during angelic number sequences, for example 1:11pm for new projects/new doorways, 4:44pm to encourage angels by your side and so on. I recommend the book, *Angel Numbers 101* by Doreen Virtue (Hay House, 2008) for more information about this.
2. Enlist the help of a numerologist to enhance your strengths and control your challenges. They will be able to give you an overall view of where you should focus your energy to become the most successful version of you.
3. Price things according to spiritual numbers. For example, $99 is great for leading by positive example, a higher perspective and altruism.
4. If you are offering a promotion or giveaway choose a number that is powerful to you. Perhaps six is your number? Why not giveaway six gift vouchers?
5. A bit trickier, but if you are yet to decide on a business name, why not have a business name with the amount of letters that equal your personal power number to bring in a flush of business success?

Intuitive knowledge

You have an innate and unique wisdom; everyone harbours this inside of themselves. It stems from being connected to everything and everyone that ever existed. The cosmic web, if you will. You may have lived many past lives (and future lives concurrently, depending on your concept of time. Have you considered that time may not be linear and occurring all at once?).

This wisdom is deep true unending and available to access anytime you want. It's hard to remember that this wisdom exists inside of us and that it's available to freely use whenever we want. Even for business knowledge. You may have cast it aside falsely believing that intuitive wisdom has no place in business. If you're connected to everything, you're connected to successful business leaders, your current and potential clientele and the wisdom of the Universe. The more you tap into this wisdom and really listen and honour it by following its guidance, the more freely it will flow.

It's human to seek inner guidance and then dismiss it as fancy or ridicule because it may not always make logical sense. Don't let that deter you.

How you can best access that wisdom is often a very personal journey but here's a number of ways you might like to try to find the most effective for you:

- automatic writing
- using oracle or tarot cards
- prayer
- casting a spell
- mandala drawing
- yoga
- meditation.

In my experience, inner wisdom, often described as intuition, is constant and persistent and has a feeling about it that isn't easily defined. It can feel like a very inspiring and elating moment or suddenly everything seems to make sense and other things fall into place surrounding it. Sometimes, it can even manifest itself as anxiety, particularly if I shove it down and don't listen to it. Often it will hit me out of the blue, when I might be distracted by something else or if I am in a calm state, like during meditation, yoga, falling asleep, in the bath, driving or reading. My very intuitive friend automatically gets covered in goose bumps whenever she hits on something pertinent for her and those around her.

If you are new to consciously using your intuition, there are many resources around including some great books that will help you learn more about this topic. If you're familiar with using your intuition, there's no reason why you can't develop this further for your business. How do you know if your idea is guided by intuition?

It's when you think of something, but it seems like you haven't thought of it before or acted on it before, and yet it feels so obvious that you could "kick yourself".

Obvious, simple, easy, flowing, exciting—these are all words that I associate with intuitive actions that are being driven by my higher self or a higher power. When something feels burdensome, heavy, blocked, confusing—then I need to look at whether they are the true pathways for me. Don't underestimate the power of time and distance when it comes to assessing whether an action is ego or soul driven. My experience is that clarity comes with time and as much detachment as I can muster—clarity rarely comes with force and overanalysing.

As humans, we rely a lot on tangible things. We don't always rely on non-tangible aspects such as emotions; our mind or ego self loves to have confirmation and proof. The Universe is well accustomed to our ways, so will confirm any message that you receive with signs and symbols, so pay attention!

The following are examples of some signs and symbols:
- number sequences (particularly if you notice this a lot)
- butterflies, birds, spiders, dragonflies etc
- words
- songs
- coincidences (known as synchronicities)
- dreams
- hearing repetitive phrases (have you heard three different people say the same thing lately?)
- seeing or hearing from someone you were just thinking about
- running into the same person frequently
- thoughts
- colours or patterns.

As an example, I am often assured that I am being looked after when the song *Heaven Let Your Light Shine Down* gets stuck in my head, seemingly from nowhere, and then I'll hear it on the radio!

Here's a quick list of what some of the animal/insect symbols could mean. They may appear in your dreams, in real life, in pictures or someone may mention them to you.

Spider: we are all one, connected together by the web of life. It also means wisdom, protection and you are on the right track.
Butterfly: transformation, emerging, the right ideas, someone in Heaven who is watching over you.
Birds: I believe that birds deliver messages. I often have various types of birds sing outside my bedroom window (of various residences) at odd hours of the day and night. I trust that my subconscious is absorbing their messages being sung to me, even though I am not fluent in bird!
Green beetles (like rain beetles etc): this is a very positive sign for your finances, if you've just asked for a specific amount of money, rest assured it's on its way to you right now. It signifies financial abundance.
Ladybirds: the bug of love! Love and romance or a positive partnership is heading your way. If you've just made a big wish,

it's about to come true.

Dragonflies: luck, seeing through an illusion, enlightenment.

Lizards: relax; soak in the experience of what you are going through. Have a break, engage in deep rest, and take things slowly and luxuriously. It's also a message to be resourceful and sturdy, rather than whimsical in your current state.

Snakes: shedding of old skin (something that no longer serves you), deception, temptation, the need to let go of fear.

Elephants: eternal wisdom and clearing of obstacles. Let the elephant guide and clear your path to success.

Rat: there is a liar in your midst!

Goldfish: success and luck. You have the Midas touch and everything you are currently doing is turning to gold!

Wolf: a stoic protector and ruthless seeker. The wolf advises you to attack what you want with vigour right now.

Lion: loyalty, a fierce protectiveness, the need to be bold and fearless.

Praying mantis: a spiritual guide, stillness, patience, the need for silence and contemplation.

Cricket/cicada: the perfect timing, doing something just for the love of it.

Bees: activity, communication, industriousness and community.

Ants: working as a team, cooperation, structure, preparation.

Scorpion:—passion, a desire to sting someone for you own protection, someone is untrustworthy.

Whale: deep perception and navigation, emotions.

Dolphin: play, nurture, joy, helping others.

Activity: why not include some animal totems in your marketing? You may like to incorporate them into your logo, in images you use or just embody their essence when undertaking a task.

What do you want?

Stop. Breathe.

Why did you start reading this book? Why do you want to promote your business? If your answer is because you feel like you should... then I suggest you hire someone to do your marketing for you, otherwise you might become resentful, neglectful and all your initial hard work will go to waste.

So! What is it you want to achieve?
More sales? More awareness? To become known as the most accurate psychic in your city? To help twenty people reach their ideal weight this year? To achieve your business' corporate goals this year by creating a community of engagement?

If you don't have clear, precise answers to this then put the book down and take a break. Go for a jog, a nap or watch some television and then come back to me when your answer is so clear that you could have it tattooed on your lower back.

'I want more sales', is a more than acceptable answer. Don't be afraid to want this.

It's not only absolutely imperative to know WHAT you want to achieve but why. Think of the "what" as your Shiva deity (clarity, knowledge, unlimited observer) and the "why" as your Shakti (power/movement/change) energy. There is no point building up a terrific social media following if you're not even sure why you're doing it.

Once you've established the "what" and the "why" then it's a great idea to identify what success will look like, so you know it when you get to it! It's nice to have this point of reflection in case our inner being isn't reflecting our outer "story". Good, measurable benchmarks could be new and regular clients, sales made, social media statistics or one new client that makes you feel alive with purpose.

Set a realistic timeframe that doesn't put pressure on you and that allows your new found skills and marketing tactics to work. That might be three months, six months, a year or two— depending on your business and the amount of time you invest in your new campaigns.

When you reach your set milestones, remember to genuinely reward yourself (and your staff). This might look like taking a full-day off, a monetary incentive or similar—something that is personal to help you feel valued. This can difficult to remember to do, especially if you are your own boss.

When people ask me if they should 'go on Twitter' or start up an Instagram account or whatever the question may be, I ask one clear question: 'what is it that you ultimately want to achieve?'

Branding

Branding is the "what" of your business. It's the way you spread your business' core message and is comprised of your look and feel (including elements such as your logo, website design, brochures etc) as well as your mission statement and how you present your business. Design and branding are paramount in marketing. It's what helps us to identify a company, organisation or business straight away. We even register companies' branding subconsciously. Branding is a way of positioning your business— it is your philosophy and it encompasses how things look, the message that the brand and business conveys and the consistency in which those things occur.

I know you're already tempted to skip this section… it's like I can read your mind! But this is one section that I urge you not to skip. We're aiming to position your business or service amongst the myriad of marketing already out there. We want to determine where it fits, where it doesn't and how to maximise that fit to your advantage.

You may create your own branding or if you hire a branding professional, you will need to provide them with a brief. Here are some things to consider:

Questions:
1. What colour or colours represent what you offer to the world?
2. What image, symbols, words or icon represents what you offer to the world?
3. Refer back to your philosophy. Do you remember it?

Tip: keep your colour scheme to less than four colours and make sure you have at least one dark tone and one light tone to contrast.

Tip: if you're having trouble visualising your logo you can also use the business naming meditation in this book.

Positioning manifest

Firstly, let's work on a positioning manifesto. This is the document that you will keep referring back to—it's your outline of what you offer so you know where you stand in the marketplace and how to keep centring yourself with your own message and to not get lost in the throng of communication.

This is a brilliant exercise to do, not just so you have it on hand should you wish to hire support to help you with your marketing or in promoting your business but it's super helpful for you to keep referring back to so you're clear about what you offer and why you offer it. Even just having it running in the back of your head will permeate through your energy to anyone you meet. If you're unclear on what it is that you do, others will be too!

Activity: set a timer for 12 minutes. Write consistently without stopping during this time. Write about your brand and what it is and what it means to you. Keep writing without stopping, even if you have to write the same thing over and over again. Once the 12 minutes are complete, review what you've written and pull out some keywords, particularly those that have been repeated. This exercise allows some ingrained knowledge about your branding that you take for granted, float to the surface. Incorporate these words in your positioning manifesto.

Activity: what emotion is tied up with your branding? Pick one and pick a strong one. Is it passion? Peace? Desire? Joy? If you're branding was a colour what would it be and why? If you haven't been using this colour for your logo and subsequent visual branding, why not?

Add what you discover to your manifesto.

What is your core service or product?
Perhaps you have more than one and that's okay because I celebrate diversity and I'm certainly not asking you to limit yourself but for the purpose of marketing and promotion I urge you to focus on two at the most. People are simple creatures and we don't cope very well with an overabundance of information thrown at us.

How to identify your core/s:
1. What do you sell the most of?
2. What are you most known for?
3. Where do your core skills, knowledge, education and training point to?
4. What is your number one (or two) passion?
5. When you fill out forms what job title do you put down? Imagine you can only use one or two words to describe what you do.
6. What do your friends tell other people that you do?

Did this process provide you with conflicting or too many answers? If you were only allowed to do two things or sell two things (if you have many products, see if you can limit it to one or two categories. For example, cosmetics and clothing) and nothing else that would sustain your desired economic status and fulfil your heart, what would they be? If these two things are not even close to what you're doing now, then you need a whole different book! You need to reconsider your career path and unequivocally follow your bliss!

Let's go back to why you're reading this book — most likely it's to increase sales or spread awareness of your business. What are the two things from your core list that you could do that will almost definitely increase your sales?

Answer the following questions after contemplating on your business. Be clear and concise and write it down so that it becomes real.

- What is your business' mission?
- What can you do for the individual?
- What can you do for society?
- What does your business currently excel at?
- What are the benefits and features of your products or services?
- What do your customers and prospects already think of

your business?

- What qualities do you want them to associate with your business?
- Where do you want your business to be in the future?

Now, distil what you have written to half or three quarters of a page, eliminating any repetition and creating short statements. You can use the following template:

Business name:
My company's/business's mission is to…
We provide…
We pride ourselves on…
Our vision is…

Remember: your brand is valuable, it's possibly more valuable than your actual business, so make sure you set it up and protect it up thoroughly.

The Four Ps
Have you heard about the four Ps of branding? Position, Promotion, Placement and Price.

Position:
This is where your business sits in the market. Consider what you do and how you do it well. Summarise it in one concise sentence, be clear and specific and. Focus on your strengths and how you can portray them in the most efficient way possible. Have you ever heard about the concept called the eleven second elevator pitch? Imagine meeting someone new in an elevator. You have eleven seconds to surmise what you do and sell your business before the elevator reaches their floor and you really need to make an impact that sticks in their mind. Your position sentence is going to be your elevator pitch. Memorise it to use anytime you meet someone new!

For example, I am an international bestselling author that has ten successful books published.
As opposed to: I am a writer.

Another example could be: I am a highly trained Reiki practitioner that has helped hundreds of clients heal their bodies and life.

Can you notice the difference? You're really selling yourself and the success you've had, rather than merely stating fact. If you're not clear on what you do best or your successes in your industry, ask a friend or colleague. It's vital that you know this for yourself, not only so you can be clear in your own mind but so that you believe your own words when you tell people and it permeates from your inner being.

Promotion:
We look at promotion as a whole throughout this book, so I'm pretty sure we've got this one covered!

Placement/place:
Placement or place refers to your physical premises: what are the benefits of where you are placed? Do you have a quiet studio surrounded by lush gardens? Then it's imperative that you promote this. Are you located in cyber land? Then promote that you can be accessed from anywhere in the world!
This "P" also relates to your place in the market. Are you the only provider of a certain product in your area? Are you a leading expert in your field? If you're unsure, do your research and/or use sweeping or broad terms such as "one of", "amongst the best/leading", "arguably" etc.

Price:
Price says a lot about what you offer. Price says a lot about what you offer. If you sell something for far too little, it creates a sense that the product or service is inferior and if you set the price too high, it will feel like it's elite and unapproachable (of course, you might decide this is where you would like to position your business). Plus, very few people may be able to afford it. When communicating price to your targeted demographics, use words that epitomise your pricing strategy. If you're on the lower end, use words like "affordable", "cost effective" and

"good value". If you're at the other end of the scale I forbid you from ever using the word "expensive" and certainly do not apologise for costing more! I have actually seen people say the following in their marketing communication: 'Yes, we may be a little bit more expensive but that's because it costs us X amount to make…' Never do this. Consumers do not care about how much it costs you to make your product or how much time you have put into it, so don't bother telling them. Instead, use words like "premium", "exclusive", "superior", "luxury", "exquisite", "high end". Here's a handy trick: to find words to use to convey your pricing position, have a look at the language that car sellers use. Cheaper cars are often billed as "economy" and "great value" and luxury cars are "prestigious". Real estate agents use similar wording.

Did you know? That less than ten per cent of Australia's population define themselves as older families/couples with high incomes and assets? Whereas over forty per cent are young singles, retirees and young families with average or low incomes. That means if you are only targeting people with a high income, the pool of people is a lot smaller.

Activity: turn your brand (not your product) into a character! Pretend you're going to insert this character into a movie, play or book, so it needs to be realistic, believable and three dimensional. They will have certain quirks, distinctive traits and be easily recognisable. Give your brand personality!

This is a great way to solidify your branding. Whenever you're unsure about whether something holds true to your branding you can just ask yourself if it is true to the character that you created in this activity.

Tip: be true to your branding as best you can. It's perfectly wonderful to be aspirational in your branding but don't have a brand that is something that your business is not and never will be.

Mission statement

If you really want to be successful in your marketing and

business, you might consider a mission statement.

A mission statement is a summary of your philosophy and what your business and you ultimately stand for. It's also a really handy marketing tool that can be used in a variety of ways— when someone asks you what you do, you can repeat it to them. It can be used on all marketing collateral—digital and hardcopy, so people automatically know what to expect from you and can connect on the same energetic level.

It's also super useful for you to keep coming back to. Anytime you have a question, challenge or are unsure of the next step, come back to your mission statement and ponder 'is what I'm planning to do in alignment with my philosophy'?

> My mission statement for Incense and Happiness is:
> Live authentically. Live creatively. Live purposefully.

It's simple but it encompasses how I expect to live, how I want others to experience life and what my whole business ethos covers. All my services and products come from one or all (mostly all) of these places.

Create your mission statement.
List your services and products using as few words as possible. Keep them to nouns (if you can) and be specific. For example: healing, coaching, massage, clothing, art therapy, tarot readings.

Now take each service and list what that service or product actually offers your /clients/customers, still keeping it to one or two word answers. For example:

Healing:
- compassion
- health
- wellbeing
- wholeness
- peace
- joy

- repair
- restore
- love

Massage:
- touch
- care
- healing
- energy
- peace
- relaxation
- happiness

You can see the process start to unfold here. Highlight the words that really mean something to you, that jump out at you or trigger an emotional response in you.

Healing:
- compassion
- health
- wellbeing
- wholeness
- peace
- joy
- repair
- restore
- love

Massage:
- touch
- care
- healing
- energy
- peace
- relaxation
- happiness

Almost like a fun story making children's game, now take the words you have highlighted and put them into a sentence or two. BUSINESS NAME aims to repair your love through compassionate touch. Or you can list the words for extra punch. Example: Compassion. Love. Repair.

You may already have a sentence or two that you know will work for your mission statement. My advice is to write it across a big piece of paper and edit it. See how many words you can reduce it by. Brevity is the key as you want people to absorb your message in a split second.

Rhythm is also an additional quality to have in your statement. Is there a way that you can make the sentence flow? Read it out loud! Practise on people and monitor their reactions. Ask someone to read it out to you. How does it sound? Clunky and complicated? Or smooth and heart warming?

I also recommend undertaking an internet search on your new mantra—your mission statement—to see if it's relatively unique. If it's used by many similar businesses, try the activity again until you come up with something fresh and meaningful.

Business name

A vital part in marketing is your branding and an imperative part of your branding is your business name. You probably have already decided on a name for your business or you may be running it under your own name. But perhaps you haven't yet or are still deciding? Or maybe, in alignment with your renewed business vision, you may be ready to change it. In which case, here are some activities to help.

Adjective and noun
Choose your favourite adjective (describing word) and your favourite noun (a person, place or thing). For example, dizzy + cat = The Dizzy Cat.

Ask Spirit!
Have you ever noticed how wonderful Spirit is at providing you

with answers and inspiration? When I created one of my writing pseudonyms I knew I wanted to use my great grandmother's first name but I couldn't come up with a suitable surname. I asked Spirit to lead the way. At the time, I was working in a bookstore and at that very moment that I was asking Spirit, I started unpacking a box of books called *Wildflower*. The cover was striking and noticeable, with an elephant on the front cover, which happens to be my favourite animal. And thus my pseudonym was born. The name felt right from that moment.

Naming meditation

Here's a meditation you may like to try if you are struggling to come up with a name or you're not sure you chose the right one. Find a comfortable space, lying or sitting down. Gently allow your eyes to close and feel your body become heavy. Notice as your feet sink deep into the floor and become so heavy you are unable to lift them. Feel your hands also become thick and heavy.

Bring your awareness to your breath. Become aware of the inhalation and the gentle pause at the end of the inhalation. Allow the body to exhale and notice the pause at the end of the exhalation.

Invite your Spirit team in to help you—whoever that is for you. Perhaps it's a passed over relative, an angel or deity or your higher self. Set your intention of finding your business name. Ask your Spirit team to help you find your business name. One that will embody your business and your essence and hold you in good stead and offer all the success you can desire plus more.

Imagine yourself entering a dense forest. The air is fresh and sweet smelling and the sun has risen only minutes ago. You can see dances of light trickling through the various greens of the trees. Notice that you are walking along a distinctive pathway. Keep following the pathway past many, many trees. Eventually, you will know to stop at a tree.

You will be guided to a specific tree. Search this tree's trunk. You'll find a carving in the tree trunk. It looks like this carving has been done with a sharp rock, or bone and it has been specifically left here for you. Notice what it says. Perhaps it is a word or a few words. Perhaps it is an image or a symbol. Trust the very first thing that you see in your mind.

Perhaps you may like to touch it. Thank the tree for showing you this message and begin your journey on the same pathway back out of the forest, holding the image from the tree in your heart. Keep slowly journeying back on that pathway until you completely leave the forest.

Come back into the room, back into your body. Notice the heaviness of your body and begin to deepen your breath. When you are ready slowly allow your eyes to open.

If you have emerged out of this meditation without a fully formed business name then don't worry! Trust that it's on its way to you now. It may appear to you in a dream, through a friend, in an overhead conversation or in a lovely surprising way like me with the book cover!

If you still haven't found your business name after a week or two, are you paying attention? Perhaps the Universe is constantly giving you clues that you are ignoring? Trust what you receive!

A demographic is a group of people that you are aiming your message towards. They are defined by their characteristics, purchasing habits and other factors.

Here are three types of demographic groups. Within each group you can further filter into more specific demographics.

Engaged group
Also known as your existing or primary group, these are the people who are already addressable and interested in what you have to offer and have knowledge of your product/service. Although smaller, this group are easier to influence. The one thing you will have to provide is a unique selling point or a reason why they should continue to choose you above their existing practitioners or suppliers.

New group
Also known as your secondary group, these people are more likely to be potential clients/customers. They may have never tried your product or service or have little or no knowledge about your business but are open to taking that step or have been referred to you but are yet to "cross that line" and make contact with you. They may also have signed up to your enews or have enquired about you in the past without taking it further.

This group may be larger but will require more energy and work to encourage them to move into the engaged group.

Hard group
This is a wide group of people, also known as the wishful or bonus group, that have no interest in your topic and are not open to learning or hearing about it and are unlikely to (however, if they do open up at some point, they automatically swap into the new group, then may convert to the engaged group). Needless to say, the return on effort (and there might be a lot of effort involved) is not worth reaching out to this group.

Your target demographic will be the people that you want to communicate directly with who are most likely to buy your service or product. This is not about excluding anyone from your marketing prowess but is about honing in on the people most likely to buy from you so you save your time and resources and get a better result.

I'm going to help you simplify this process so that you will find a useful and helpful way to use this knowledge, rather than overwhelm you with possibilities. My intention is not to dumb this down for you but to find a way of melding common sense and technical marketing knowledge in a useable and workable concept. By all means, if you feel guided to, do some extensive research on demographics and how to identify and reach them. You can even go so far as to boil it down to a sample person based on all the median research that has been done. A lot of larger consumer companies do this, so they know who they are targeting and can personify their demographic in the hope of really speaking to them.

Remember: don't fall into a seductive trap of thinking that your product or service is best marketed to everyone. It is simply not the case that your product or service will be wanted or accommodates everyone, so it's better to maximise your time and effort and really hone in on the target demographic that will make your business thrive. Be aware that this might only be five people that purchase a hundred thousand dollars worth of product from you each year. Or it might be twenty thousand people that buy ten dollars worth of product from you each month.

How to identify who is in your existing and new groups:
- use existing knowledge
- use your inner knowing
- collect and collate data on your existing clients
- base your demographic on people who are in the same field as you (some of this information may already be available for your industry, check out some of the

resources below).

Resources for finding data:
- Australian Bureau of Statistics
- University journal databases
- Marketing magazines and websites
- Data collection agencies (sometimes you have to pay for information and reports). There are companies specifically set up to curate this data for people to access.
- Google Scholar
- The internet is wonderful, of course, but there may be a lot of information you have to wade through. Ensure you put aside enough time to do so.

Remember: sometimes this data can appear to be quite academic, so if that isn't your strength, have tolerance with yourself as you sift through and extract the information that is most helpful to you. You are learning a new skill here, so be patient and encouraging with yourself and enjoy the journey and the sense of achievement.

Here is a simplified example of demographics broken down into three groups.

BUSINESS NAME sells an organic cotton clothing range in a dedicated retail store in Byron Bay. They also sell their range online, via their website.

Primary demographic
Females aged from 20 to 45 years, who live in suburban areas and mostly come from Victoria and New South Wales. They prefer to buy their clothing in-store but will often research the product thoroughly online first.

They go to yoga and meditation classes, prefer to shop and eat organic and most of the group are mothers and work for themselves in some capacity.

Secondary demographic

This cohort includes the primary group's partners, parents, friends or children that buy for this group and might also include wholesalers that act as a middle man for BUSINESS NAME's product.

Tip: treasure your wholesalers as they will be doing the hard, "on the ground" sales work for you.

Bonus/wild card

Maybe you have a dream that your business reaches the over 50s market. Perhaps there needs to be some alterations to your product or service to suit this demographics' lifestyle (and you'll know what that looks like because you've done your research!) Perhaps your product or service already suits this group but you need to alter your branding so it really speaks to them. In this example, you might consider creating an "Over 50s" range with more classic branding.

Tip: to successfully communicate with any of your demographics, find out what they want through customer segregation. You can't do this by guessing or assuming what they want. You can do this by asking them (perhaps as an incentivised survey) or by doing your research and monitoring people's behaviours, trends and attitudes towards other products and services. See the section on focus groups for more information.

Template

Here's a very basic template to identify your target market by creating customer profiles. Fill one out for the primary and secondary groups including their median statistics. Creating a profile for your bonus group is optional.

Age:
Gender:
Location:
Marital and family status:
Who they live with:

Income:
Occupation:
Interests/hobbies:
Spending habits:
What products/services they value in their life:
How they make decisions:
Social media habits:
Words that make them interested in a product/service:
How they hear about new products/services:
Best way to communicate to them:
Find out specifically where they spend most of their time online
(a certain blog/website, Facebook, email etc):

Remember: people's behaviours and wants change regularly, so you will need to reassess who your target demographics are at least once a year.

You may already see how this information is helpful in speaking directly to your customer or potential customer. If we revisit our example above, most of BUSINESS NAME'S primary group go to yoga and are parents. This opens up countless possibilities of how you can reach this demographic. For example, advertise in a yoga magazine or at a yoga class, run a yoga mat giveaway competition, word your promotions towards people who are busy and need easy to care for clothing.

Did you know: that expectant or new parents are nearly three times more likely to search the internet than non parents? (Search Engine Land, August, 2014)

'The aim of marketing is to know and understand the customer so well the product or service fits him and sells itself,' Peter Drucker.

Market research

In traditional marketing, companies often set up a focus group. This is a random selection of people (often paid) to provide their opinion on a service or product. Television and television commercials still use this method of collecting information a lot. This is an effective way of monitoring people's reactions to the product in real life and seeking out how the product can be improved or how it can most effectively be communicated.

If you want to set up a focus group, be prepared to seek outside of your usual business or social circles. You can target universities and colleges, business communities, libraries and councils to help recruit people. When recruiting for people, ensure you are completely transparent about what you are asking and set a specific time, date and time allocation for the focus group. Be prepared also to offer them a reward for their time. Cash, food or discount vouchers often work well, as does an exchange of their time for your service or product. Be thoroughly prepared with what information you want to find out from the focus session long before it occurs. It's a good idea to hire a third party to conduct the session as it will need to be rigorously managed and some negative things could be said about your business and people want to feel comfortable that they can express their truth. There are companies you can hire who do this professionally.

If you don't have the resources to set up a focus group then an easy and cheap way of collecting mass data is by creating a survey. Online platforms such as Survey Monkey are great for this. You will need to pay a subscription if you wish to ask over ten questions.

Unfortunately, people resent doing something for nothing so offer people an incentive to complete the survey. That could be a discount voucher or a lucky prize draw for a larger prize. Don't forget to keep your branding consistent with your survey and always have a way of connecting it back to your website or social media platforms.

Remember: this is a valuable opportunity to collect data, so make sure you don't waste it. The more you understand your customer, the more you can give them what they want in a way they want.

Social media marketing

It's undeniable that social media can enhance business, particularly if it's done well. Small to medium businesses can increase their revenue by more than ten percent, as revealed by a 2013 survey, completed by MYOB. The survey revealed that 28 per cent of SMEs using social media reported an increase in revenue, compared to an average of 18 per cent across all SMEs.

What does engagement mean?

No you don't have to marry anyone! Engagement means commenting on your posts, 'liking', sharing your posts or referencing you or your business in other people's posts. It also means retweeting, replying to tweets or resharing blog posts. Engagement is the absolute key to effective marketing because engagement makes sales, shouting your messages at someone doesn't increase sales. Customers want to be a part of something and seek out genuine and meaningful online interactions.

> **'People don't buy what you do, they buy why you do it,'**
> **Simon Sinek.**

80 – 10 – 10 rule

My favourite rule for social media is the 80 – 10 – 10 rule. It refers to the ratio of content that social media experts have come to the collective conclusion that you should post to be most effective in ensuring audience engagement without ticking off your followers. Social media is about the people you are connecting to. It's not really about you or your business despite being one of the most powerful tools to promote your business and service.

80 per cent information/entertainment
This is a big chunk of what you post and should be thought through carefully. This can include links to useful blogs (including your own), pictures of cats (yes, really!), info graphics, fun facts, short recipes, informative videos and so on.

10 per cent engagement
As we have just discussed engagement is imperative in social

media marketing so be sure to get a conversation flowing. Pretend that Facebook is a dinner party and you're inviting a new conversation to start.

Take ten minutes now to write down a list of conversational questions that you can ask your Facebook followers. Remember to encourage their responses and reply with warmth when people do respond. Here are some starter questions that you can use:
- 'Where is the best massage you've ever had?'
- 'What word do you use to describe God?'
- 'Where's the best place you've ever visited?'

10 per cent promotion
Keep your sales and promotional posts to a minimum. I believe this rule refers to raw promotional posts that have no added value for the follower. It's still important to share what you do so there's no reason why you can't combine your promotional posts with entertainment or information as long as it's relevant.

The best rule for social media is to have a play! Trial and error is a great way to learn and because of social media's newness to the world, that is how a lot of people who have quickly become deemed experts have had to learn in a very short space of time. The best thing is that we have developed a community where people are willing to share their social media knowledge.

Social media policy

A social media policy is a guide of conduct for social media for people who work for you. It provides them with your expectations as to how they behave on the social media that will have an impact on your business. This is particularly important if people share the social media duties for your business.

It's a great idea to implement a social media policy into your workplace if you have several employees. The people you hire can be the greatest asset and promotional tool for your business. Make sure you clearly defined the rules for them, well before disaster occurs.

You can read Coca Cola's social media policy here: http://www.coca-colacompany.com/stories/online-social-media-principles

You can find Intel's here: http://www.intel.com/content/www/us/en/legal/intel-social-media-guidelines.html
Intel has three clear rules of engagement for their employees: disclose, protect and use common sense. These are great flash words to remember when posting anything online.

Blogging

Before you start a web blog [blog] it is best to be prepared. Be sure to complete off all the things on the checklist below before you start the step by step section.

- Planner template
- Have you read the whole blog chapter in this book?
- Do you have at least two blog posts ready to post?
- Do you have a list of blog topics that you will be writing in the near future?
- Have you established a business or a blog name?
- Have some images ready — of yourself, logo, pictures relative to posts, etc
- The copy for the About, Contact, (you may skip this step if your website already has these pages and your blog is linked to your website)
- Examples of leading blogs
- A working email address for your WordPress login
- A username for your WordPress login— minimum of four characters and that only includes lowercase letters and numbers.
- A password for your WordPress login

Why blog?
Blogging is an excellent way to contribute to your digital marketing plan. It's a way of sharing content with the online community that will increase the amount of people who are interested in what you have to say and what you can offer the world in terms of products and/or services.

Blogging also:
- creates exposure for your brand/business
- entices new clients/customers
- provides confidence and instils trust in your consumers that you are knowledgeable about your industry
- encourages/motivates you to write and be creative more/regularly
- offers instant satisfaction of seeing your work published

and accessible instantly
- creates an opportunity for people to provide feedback on your writing
- refines your writing skills
- can lead to career/job opportunities in the future
- connects you with a larger community
- is a learning opportunity
- has potential to earn you money
- is relatively easy and rapid
- can reach a worldwide audience
- is free/low cost.

Blogging platform

A blogging platform is the internet based software that you will be using. I find the following the easiest to navigate and the most intuitive to set up and use:
WordPress
Blogger
Tumblr
Weebly

WordPress

Because of its diversity, WordPress is a great blogging and website platform. I'm going to run through the steps for starting a blog on WordPress but if you find that you would prefer another platform, most internet "how to" guides are useful and each platform has their own help guide which is usually designed for people who have never blogged before.

1. Go to WordPress.com
2. Click "Get Started"
3. Type in your email address (that you want associated with logging in to your blog), username and password
4. Choose the name of your blog (all one word, no spaces) —it will let you know if it's available or not.
5. By now, WordPress will probably be asking you to verify your new site via a link sent to you via email. Once you have done that, you are ready to go!

If you don't have a domain name already, then you may like to choose domain hosting via WordPress, which costs about $18 per year. Alternatively, you can use the free option which will require you to have a sub address which includes "WordPress" in the URL. So it may look like this:
www.yourbusiness.WordPress.com
If you were to pay for your own domain hosting (usually between $10 and $20 per year in Australia) it would look like this: www.yourbusiness.com

If you are registering your own domain, the hosting company (WordPress or other) will offer you an additional service of privacy settings, where for a nominal fee they can hide your personal details that are linked to your domain. This is a personal choice and stops the lay person web searching your residential address and phone number. But know that anything you put into the internet, is discoverable by those who have more advanced skills, should they want to.

You can get a cheaper domain through hosting sites outside of WordPress but it does offer a very simple process of matching up your domain to your new WordPress site.

The following are some common web hosting services you might like to use:
- Zuver
- Servers Australia
- Bluehost
- Dreamhost
- GoDaddy

I recommend using the free WordPress package option (at least for now), you can always upgrade to the bigger packages at a later stage and they probably aren't necessary unless you are running a website that requires a lot of storage space. You can also have as many WordPress blogs/sites as you like!

To recap:
Plan: free beginner

Domain hosting: choose a company (or use WordPress to host)
Platform: WordPress
WordPress.com or WordPress.org?

WordPress.org is the one to use if you are self-hosting (that means you've bought a domain via an external company, such as Zuver etc).

WordPress.com is fine for beginners and people who don't need a website with too much complexity. If you have some technical know-how or know someone that does that can help you, and you intend to have lots of extras on your website (for example. you would like to run an online course, use more plugins, have your own custom design, discussion forums etc), then it is worth exploring WordPress.org.

WordPress use the analogy that WordPress.com is like renting a house and WordPress.org is like buying a house—you can make all the alterations and modifications to suit you but you're also responsible if things break or go awry.

It's worth noting that whilst you can still sell easily on a WordPress.com site, if online selling is your primary goal, then it's advised to use WordPress.org.

Dashboard
In the top left hand corner, there will be an icon of the Earth. Hover on that and a drop down menu will reveal a few items, one of which will be the dashboard. Click on this and let's explore! Much like a car dashboard, this area holds all the functions of your site.

You'll notice a very handy video pop up as soon as you connect to your dashboard. If you are new to blogging, there is pretty much no better way to learn your way around WordPress than straight from the horse's mouth!

Once you've watched the tutorial video, I recommend that you work on the visual aspect of your blog first.

Theme

Choose a theme via the dashboard. Appearance > theme. Select your theme and click Preview to see what it looks like and "Activate", once you have decided. You can customise it by clicking Customize.

Choose a theme that represents your business and blog and is consistent with your branding.

WordPress has an array of themes to choose from, some are free and some with a fee attached. The free ones are great and customisable but sometimes you might want something a bit more unique or you have seen a design that you just have to have that will do your business justice and then it's worth paying for your theme. Themes can generally cost approximately $30 - $130 for their lifetime. Their creators will often create updates for the theme (ironing out any bugs, adding more options etc — much like when you update your iPhone apps) and you'll be alerted when you login to your WordPress blog as to when you need to do this. Often, it only involves clicking "update".

Remember: your logo will need to be prominent, ideally in the top header/banner, so be sure to choose colours and design that will complement your logo and branding.

Tip: don't be lured in by the gorgeousness of the paid themes, free themes can look just as effective. You can also pay designers to create customised themes for you too.

Don't forget that the majority of people will be viewing your blog on their phone or tablet, so you need to make sure that it looks okay on these devices too. When you are customising the theme, there is a little icon that displays a computer, phone and tablet image and by clicking on each one, it will give you a preview of what it will look like on each device.

Pages

Pages are the static pages of text that can be chosen from the menu. One page will contain your blog posts and more often than not, this will default as your home page, although you can change this in the dashboard. It's up to you which page you choose as your landing page (where people "land" when they type in your web address) but I recommend that it be your home page or your blog posts, which may be one and the same.

You may choose to have a home page that acts as an introductory text, especially if you are combining your website and blog into the one platform.

To add pages to your menu (or your menu may reside at the top or side of your page), go to: Dashboard> Appearance> Menu.

Posts
Posts are the rolling, usually reverse chronological order boxes of text that you will be regularly updating. This is where your blog posts will go. All your posts will sit on one page (unless you direct them to various pages, based on categories—this is an option for the more advanced users or the more complex site).

Private posts
You can password protect any post that you wish. This may be a useful tool in case you have content that only some people are privy to; maybe it's private information that you would like to keep for your friends or your regular clients. Or maybe you have a subscription service where people pay to access some of your content. WordPress has a plugin for more advanced users such as Membership, which helps to organise subscription services like a lot of modern news services offer these days or Coursepress which allows you to run online courses. There is undoubtedly a plugin for everything you can think of. Try having a search through the plugin directory (you'll need WordPress.org to install plugins).

Copyright
Copyright belongs to you if it's your own work. You are automatically granted copyright – you don't have to do anything. On the other side of the coin—do not plagiarise! You'll ruin

your reputation at the click of a button. That applies for uploading other people's images to your website or blog. You must fully accredit the creator of the image. Copyright Australia is a useful resource for all copyright information.

Blogging tips
- Write what you know. Do you have a particular interest that you know a lot about? For example, cooking, photography, raising chickens, vegetable gardening, ballet, reviews (e.g. movies, albums, restaurants).
- Choose your genre: fiction, non-fiction, poetry, instructional, review/opinion, experimental.
- Do something different. Write about something that hasn't been written a lot about yet. People are always looking for new and interesting content on the web.
- Write what interests you, things you are passionate about to ensure you don't burn out.
- Before you start blogging, make sure you have a long list of possible articles so you don't run out of steam.
- Compose your post/article using the "pyramid formula" (but include a good resolve or summary).
- Keep your blog posts concise and easy to read.
- Proofread and spell check.
- A heading and a first introductory sentence that draws readers in is imperative.
- Don't be shy about offering your opinion or discussing the big, controversial issues.
- Include short sentences, bullet points, hyperlinks, bold keywords and make your post easy to scan and improve your SEO (search engine optimisation—more about SEO later).
- Research other blogs to see what works and what doesn't.
- Most good blogs have a list of categories.
- Define your audience beforehand; who do you want to write to?
- Remember that blogging is like running a small business. Expect to treat it that way and since you

already run your own business, you already know how!
- If you want a conversation, it helps to converse!
- Offer people a community; make them feel part of a group by encouraging interaction between each other, not just between you and them.
- Have a clear and consistent voice throughout your blog. It's best to start with one that you are able to maintain, one close to your own way of speaking and communicating is a way to ensure it is consistent.
- The best thing you can do for your blog is create engaging, strong content.

Headlines
Have a compelling heading for each blog post. Make sure it's a bit of a tease and that people will want to click on it and read more. Include why someone absolutely must read this post; explain why it will change their life/business/mind etc. The headline must be about the reader and how it can benefit them. For example, *How Garlic Will Make You Lose Weight*

'With titles, it's best to under promise and over deliver. So if you're choosing between uber-compelling and accurate, choose accuracy every time,' Corey Eridon, Hubspot Marketing Blog.

Here are some things to add that will create punch in your headline:
- alliteration
- anything that is intriguing
- some urgency
- strong language/words—not necessarily swear words but clear, powerful words
- power words—words like tyranny (thanks Churchill), warning, eye opening, surprising.

A great headline should make a reader curious and want more. Here are some types of headlines that have proven themselves to work time and time again:
- problems that need solving

- warning/alert
- the art of or mastery of a topic
- timesaving or life hacks
- questions
- shockers/hoaxes/lies
- take control of…
- banish [topic] forever
- things people hate
- number of things, e.g., Five Ways To…
- here's something a "trusted person" won't tell you (i.e. doctor)
- little known facts
- what [event or person] can teach us about [topic]
- how to…

Do you know? Headlines with approximately six words tend to have the highest click through rates.

How to write a blog post:
In the spiritual and wellbeing realm there are endless topics to explore and write about. There are many fascinating topics to share with a broad audience that may be new information to a lot of your readers. It would be rare that you struggle for content—especially as Spirit is very generous in giving you frequent downloads.

My experience is that a lot of spiritual blogs have interesting information but don't convey it in the best possible way.

Here are some guidelines:
1. Keep your post 300—500 words long. We have a short concentration span, particularly when it comes to the internet so brevity is the key! Try and condense your idea into less than a page and it will be easier to digest and more likely to grab hold of the reader. If you are unable to convey what you want to in a limited amount of words, split it into parts and add a 'to be continued' clause at the end of your post.
2. Proofread. If you spell correctly and use correct terms

and correct grammar it will give your information more credibility and stand out. It's worth hiring a proofreader/writer. Why not trade services with a writer friend? Trust me—writers always need a massage or Reiki or a treatment of some kind.

3. Pyramid format.
4. What is your point? Don't waffle! Spirit is great at giving information and insights but it is not always provided in a logical order for humans to comprehend. You're the lucky one that has been chosen to interpret and present it in a form that everybody can understand. See below for how to write a blog post.
5. Leave posts for a day or two (if the content is not time dependent) and reread a couple of times. Check that they make sense and that you have proofread with utmost scrutiny.
6. Do you research? It's not hard now with the internet. Remember to attribute quotes to people who have said /written them, reference facts, statistics and resources.

Utilise footnotes, hyperlinks and traditional referencing systems. A quick internet search will guide you through these. Invest in doing a short grammar course.

Content ideas

Here's some ideas of what you could blog about, keep adding your own suggestions to this list:
- opinion pieces
- "how to" guide
- tutorials
- recipes
- industry knowledge/expertise
- explanatory post
- tips and hints
- what I've learnt
- history or philosophy of your chosen modality/industry
- interviews/Q&A session with key industry leaders or staff members

Having trouble coming up with content? Try this fun online tool: http://750words.com/

How to write an opinion piece blog post.
Pick one firm idea or topic. Try not to introduce multiple ideas into the one blog post—save them for separate posts. It's also a great idea to have a concrete idea, your readers want to know what they are reading about—not something that meanders with no firm foundation (we are creatures of security).

Have a resolve. Again, we love our security so ensure you have a decent resolve. My pet hates are posts that finish with 'I don't know, what do you think?' Whilst I encourage engagement, I want what I'm reading to have a firm opinion—otherwise, what is the point in reading it?
Imagine if your favourite movie didn't have a satisfying resolve—how traumatising!

Here's a formula you can use for writing an opinion piece:

Topic: Red is the best colour

   Heading: Red Will Change Your Life and Here's Why…

1. Intro: I believe that red is the best colour
2. Signposts: Here are the three reasons why I think it is the best colour, reason one, two and three.
3. Reason one expanded. Include a statistic, quote, example or anecdote to support your reasoning.
4. Reason two expanded. Include a statistic, quote, example or anecdote to support your reasoning.
5. Reason three expanded. Include a statistic, quote, example or anecdote to support your reasoning.
6. Surmise and conclude.

Is this reminding you of a writing an essay at school, university or college? It's a very similar format. Except you get to write about what you want and the only mark you get will be how your readers respond to it.

Tip: If you are like me (and probably most of the world) and you create your blog content initially in Word, there is an important step you must remember! Word automatically creates a set of formatting which is not compatible with web based programs, such as WordPress. I'll be honest here and say that I have no idea why and being a web coder is for people who are far more intelligent and patient than I am. All I know is that it is quite important. So make sure you press the button that has a "T" on it, which will strip your text of formatting, before you paste your text into WordPress from MS Word. Don't forget that you'll have to manually add the formatting (bold, italics etc) once you've pasted the content into the blog post.
Or you can use this: http://word2cleanhtml.com/

Blog planner template

Topic/s	
Title	
Target audience (i.e. gender, age, location, their interests, their lifestyle)	
What will the style/tone of your blog be?	
What is the purpose of your blog?	
What categories could your blog have?	
If you start to run out of ideas, where can you gain inspiration? (e.g. newspapers, bookstores, friends)	
Why people will choose to read your blog/point of difference?	
How many posts per week?	
Length of each post	
What images will you include?	

How will you spread the word about your blog?	
What will your first couple of posts be about?	
What do you want your readers to get out of reading your blog?	

Here's the blog planner template as an example with answers:

Topic/s	A review of every restaurant in Adelaide.
Title	Gobbling up the City
Target audience (i.e. gender, age, location, their interests, their lifestyle)	People who live in and around Adelaide. People aged 18 – 45 years, of both genders, who dine out frequently and appreciate nice food.
What will the style/tone of your blog be?	Informal, with an undertone of authority, providing an opinionated stance. It will be an objective, unbiased, fair review on the experiences that the blogger directly encounters.
What is the purpose of your blog?	To inform readers of the various types of restaurants in Adelaide and the kind of service, food, atmosphere and experience they provide.
What categories could your blog have?	Service, cleanliness, wine, food (this could be divided into sub-categories – entrée, main, dessert, vegetarian, chicken etc), atmosphere, suburbs, cuisine
If you start to run out of ideas, where can	Other blogs, newspaper reviews, television shows, recipe books,

you gain inspiration? (e.g. newspapers, bookstores, friends)	parents, friends, the internet, talk to people in the industry
Why people will choose to read your blog/point of difference?	Because it will be an unbiased view of restaurants, coming from an 18 year old female (rather than the typical 50 year old restaurant reviewer)
How many posts per week?	Two posts per week.
Length of each post	Between two hundred and four hundred words each.
What images will you include?	Photos of the food, restaurant, logo, staff, blogger eating the food
How will you spread the word of your blog?	Comment on similar blogs, use social media outlets, tell people about it, tell restaurants involved, approach local media
What will your first couple of posts be about?	I will start by eating at my favourite restaurant and talking about my favourite dish there. I might like to introduce the blog and its intention, although this can be done in the "About" section.
What you want your readers to get out of reading your blog?	An idea of where to eat in Adelaide and what experience they can expect. I would like my blog to be the 'go to' guide for eating in Adelaide.

Tip: who do you want to emulate? Gather at least six examples of other blogs that display a quality that you want your blog to emulate. Remember to look at their content, design, readability and how effective the blog is as a marketing tool.

Blog promotion

You've written an informative and moving piece. Now people should read it! How will you promote your blog post? Use your social media platforms first and foremost!

Post via your Facebook
Ensure you've chosen an eye catching image and either insert it into your blog post directly or upload it to the accompanying Facebook status.

Post via Twitter
Don't stop at once. Tweet it the day you post it, then a few days later, then in a few months to remind people that it's there or to introduce new followers to it. If a timely topic has presented itself in the news etc, it's also a good time. Remember to use hashtags in your tweet that are pertinent to the blog post's topic.

Post via LinkedIn, Google+, Instagram, Yelp… anywhere you are online! Don't post all at once, spread your posts out over a period of time.
Grab "pull quotes" from your blog post when posting via your other social media platforms. These are significant sentences or quotes that will intrigue potential readers and make them want to click and read the whole post. When promoting via your enews, you can include the first couple of sentences and then recommend readers to 'read more' (hyperlink the article to these words).

Comment on other blogs. This can be a fun (warning: time sucking) activity. Spend an afternoon researching other blogs and leaving thoughtful, genuine and personalised comments. Popping a 'great blog, really enjoyed it', in the comments is going to attract nobody's attention. Comment on what you learnt from the blog, ask a question or share an experience. If you have blogged on something similar, you can always include a link politely asking the blog owner to read your post on a similar or additional topic. Remember to extend your blog commenting to people you want to become your client/customer, not just anyone in the same industry or someone doing the same things as you.

This may require you to go outside your industry to people who work in quite different fields. Blog commenting is just like commenting in real life—be respectful, polite and genuine.

This is my favourite suggestion because it's also a lot of fun but set yourself a timer because you could end up doing this for hours!
Find other similar blogs out there in the beautiful big cyber world and start commenting! A lot of commenting space on other people's blog offers the opportunity to share a link to your own blog. Or you may like to include the link yourself in the comment. Ensure that your comment is relevant to the post or you will be considered spam. No one likes spam.
Find a post that is discussing a similar comment and add something of value. Don't just say "great post".
For example, 'Thanks for sharing that information about kale. Like you, I have used it in smoothies but find that my favourite place to use it is in face masks—believe it or not! I've written about it here if you would like to check it out: www.blogpostlink.com

'Blogs and reviews continue to influence buying decisions, with over half of social media users (55%) reading reviews before making a purchase...' Sensis Social Media Report 2015.

Include in your emails
If you email a lot of people why not include a blog link in your email signature? For example:
Vanessa Jones
Writer
Phone number
(Website) www.jonesthewriter.com
(Blog) www.jonesthewriterblog.com. [Not a real link because I've added my blog to my website]

Responding to the media
If your blog post is responding to a newsworthy piece – ensure

you do so immediately. And by immediately, I really mean immediately! Within the hour! By the time tomorrow's sun emerges, news from today is barely relevant.

Many intuitive and sensitive people can find media quite toxic and heavy at times and there is potential to absorb a lot of negativity this way but you may like to keep abreast of current news affairs in terms of marketing opportunities to promote your work. You may have written a piece about immunisation recently (ensure you've written it well and your argument is well constructed, particularly when dealing with controversial topics) and a new development or spokesperson has made the news. This might be a great opportunity for you to share your views— either in the comments sections or by contacting the relevant media outlet and advising that you have written a piece, if they are interested.

Blog launch
What is a more fun than to host a blog (or website) launch! You can do this in the physical or digital space. If it's in the physical, offer nibbles and drinks or a free service or product to entice people to come. Ensure you have some marketing collateral (such as a flyer or business card) with the blog URL on it for people to take away and refer back to. If you have the budget, why not get some merchandise made up—people look at mouse pads or fridge magnets a number of times per day, increasing the likelihood of them remembering your blog or website exists.

Guest blogging
Guest blogging is a great way to increase your audience. Why not approach someone in your field (or in a completely opposite field in order to reach a different audience) and offer to write a post for them? Generally, you will be rewarded non fiscally by being linked back to your own blog. This is great, particularly if this person already has a generous following. Remember to exercise respect and adhere to their guidelines, wish and prerogative to say no.
This is the digital equivalent of presenting a speech at someone else's business—remember to present yourself in a way that

displays you (and the person you are blogging for) in the best light.

Do your research and find a blog that is similar to your field and that you can genuinely feel you can add value to. Perhaps you can offer an alternative view of an opinion they blogged about last week or further insight into something they have touched on.

Here is a cold call template letter you can use to approach someone you would like to guest blog for.

Dear <blogger name>
I have been reading <correct name of their blog> for <number> of months and I really enjoy what you have to offer.
My favourite posts are <post one> and <post two> because <one or two reasons why they touched you>.
Do you offer the opportunity of guest blogging? If so, what are your guidelines for doing so?
I would love to write a post for your blog about <topic—be as clear as you can> and I can have it to you by <date>.I would be honoured to write for such a distinguished blog that has such a supportive established following.
Please feel free to view my blog: <insert hyperlink to your own blog.>

I look forward to hearing from you soon.

Regards
<Your name>

Here are some tips on guest blogging:

1. Make sure you have at least half a dozen blog posts on your own site before approaching someone to guest blog. They will need to have some samples of your writing to refer to in order to decide if you are a good fit for their site.
2. If you haven't been following and reading their blog lately, wait a bit and become familiar with their work and site.

3. It's their prerogative to edit you as they see fit but if it's too much work they won't bother putting your content (blog post) on their site. It's best not to present them with something sloppy and riddled with errors.
4. Don't be timid about approaching bloggers from overseas or from seemingly opposite industries—this might be the audience that responds well to what you have to offer. Of course, if your service is strictly local (for example, massage) you might want to only focus on other local bloggers.
5. Don't forget to send a thank you email to the blogger for posting your words and read and respond (politely) to any comments left on your post. It is also courteous to promote your piece on their blog via your own channels.
6. Keep your blog name the same or similar to your business name. It's best to keep things as easy as possible for your readers (who are one step away from being your clients) by keeping consistent branding.
7. Make sure your blog post titles are attention grabbing for use in tweets and Facebook posts, just like you would for your own blog.
8. When you send them the final copy, ensure you include a short biography (100 words maximum) and a link to your own site. They may also request a headshot or relevant image. Be prepared and have these things ready to go.

When to blog
One of the great things about blogs is that you can write up your posts all at once and then schedule them to publish at certain times. If you're one of those all or nothing type of people (I definitely am) you may like to spend a day or two writing a month's worth of posts.

I know that you want someone to tell you that you must post at this specific time about this specific topic but it's going to be a case of experimentation for a little while to see what invites engagement and readers the most. It's more important to get your promotion right than the actual time of posting your blog piece. Content is more important than frequency. Really good thought provoking or informative material is better than posting repetitive prose every day. Consistency and rhythm is another important factor. People like to know what to expect. The bottom line is, if you can't commit to more than one post a month, then blogging probably isn't for you. If you still enjoy writing and getting your message out there it is worth exploring other options. You can write that ebook, create an audio book or do a series of video clips or in person presentations to share your message.

Remember: spread your promotion across all your various social media platforms (be creative with Instagram and Pinterest if you have them).

Remember: don't be afraid to shake up your schedule if your intuition suggests something better. The time of promoting the post via your social media platforms will ultimately be more important than the time of posting.

Tip: posting your content during the day might be best as more people are online but will have more "noise" to compete with.

Tip: it's more important to focus on when you promote your blog piece than when you post it. For example, make sure you're promoting the link via Facebook during Facebook's high traffic times.

Helpful books on blogging:
Problogger by Darren Rowse and Chris Garrett
How to Make Money with Your Blog by Duane Forrester and Gavin Powell
Blogging for Dummies by Brad Hill

Blogging by your star sign

Aries
You are adventurous, opinionated and somewhat aggressive, so you may lean towards picking a fight through your blog pieces. You're a wise thinker but err towards being impulsive. Being the first star sign, you'll want to have done things first or not at all. You're not even reading this, are you Aries? You've already gone off to write your blog!

Taurus
As a bull, you have the determination to succeed and your persistence will ensure that this happens, your blog has longevity and your audience will be built up over years rather than enjoying an initial burst and peak in your first couple of months. You'll enjoy doing this if it's done the right way; your way.

Gemini
You're busy and inquisitive and you'll enjoy the interaction and engagement that you will invite through your words. You are intelligent and cerebral, so you will present well thought out blog pieces but be careful they don't become lengthy due to your love of long explanations. Editing is the key.

Cancer
Since you love your cosy home environment, you will have plenty of time to spend blogging, from the couch of your nest. You're highly emotional, which will see you composing highly emotive and passionate pieces. This is a great motivator to write but remember to edit and reinforce your emotional pleas with facts, research, stats and/or quotes. There seem to be many cancers in the spiritual and complementary therapies industry.

Leo
Accompanied by your authoritative and bolshy nature, you love to shine your light into the world. Blogging may not satisfy your desire to be well known and recognised so you may enjoy teaming your blog with videos, Twitter and media appearances. You're self-expressive and creative, which are great traits for

marketing—especially in marketing yourself.

Virgo
Perfectionism tendencies could hamper you from just pushing "publish" or "send" (or delete) and you may find yourself deliberating too long. Sometimes, it's important to just get your word out there, even if everything isn't in place first. You'll be great at bringing in facts and logic into your posts due to your critical nature and your knack for organisation and scheduling will be a really useful tool and will ensure that blogging doesn't become a drag for you. Just write—stop waiting for your thoughts to be organised enough first.

Libra
You beautifully balanced thing, you. You will most likely see either sides (or many) to an argument, which can promote a balanced view but may leave your audience unable to solidify their opinion. Feel free to pick a side to fight for occasionally, let that inner bias roam free.

Scorpio
Given that you are honest, have a penchant for the taboo and taking things to the limits, you may want to be hyperaware of your audience. Take a breath, reread your piece and remove or reduce the venom before you hit "post". Your diligent research skills are a useful trait.

Sagittarius
Oh darling idealists! When you allow things to flow to you, you do better than striving. You favour understanding, so you'll present what you truly know to be truth, which will come across splendidly. You look towards stimulating conversations and you have a healthy sense of optimism—remember not to bite off more than you can chew.

Capricorn
Capricorns are hard workers, practical (you probably don't even believe in astrology), ambitious and matter of fact. It's okay for you to pepper your posts with emotion occasionally, as trite as it

may seem to you. This will foster a connection between you and your readers. If you aim big, you'll undoubtedly achieve the "big picture" stuff. You are also quite resilient against criticism or opposing ideas if you come against it.

Aquarius

You guys are sensitive, which you cover up with a mask. You favour easy conversation, forward thinking and unique ideas and like to express ground breaking concepts or grand ideals. That's more than okay but present it with quality research and reduce the lofty terms that you may be inclined to use. Given that you are so artistic, intuitive and broadminded; you may enjoy expressing your blog in the medium of visual art rather than words or a mixture of both.

Pisces

Hello? Pisces? Are you there? You lovely dreamers have a desire for the impossible, mythical and esoteric. You favour complexity and imagination. You might prefer to write creative prose or poetry to present your ideas rather than nonfiction articles. You're very psychic so your posts may be guided or downloaded by Spirit. Be sure to edit thoroughly.

Enewsletter

An electronic newsletter [enews] is a great marketing tool, especially if you don't yet have a blog. Enews are great for nurturing your new group into your engaged group and funnelling sales because their conversion rate from reader to buyer is very high.

The benefits of sending out a regular enews include:
1. Information is delivered directly to your subscribers' inbox so it'll make it harder to miss and scroll past. Things can get lost in the hectic social media world.
2. It can be interactive and easily incorporates links to your website, social media platforms and other content.
3. It's incredibly cost efficient.
4. People automatically pay more attention and heed to emails because more often than not, they contain direct and important information, whereas social media feeds contain general information that's spouted to everyone and our tendency is to scroll past scanning for keywords or images that are relevant to us at that time.
5. It's more static and has a longer lifespan. It could potentially stay in your inbox (and your eyesight) for a week or more, whereas Facebook posts may only be in your vicinity for half a day at most and a tweet may hang around for thirty seconds, if you're lucky!
6. It has the ability to contain more information and the ability to connect all sources of information in the one spot. It's regular, often arriving at the same time and day which creates anticipation, expectation and habit for your readers.

Your website platform or client/customer relationship management [CRM] tool may already include a mail program you can use but I recommend MailChimp. It's easy to navigate and free for the basic level and it works really well for me and whilst I encourage you to find one that suits you the best, I'll be mainly referencing MailChimp in this book. Here are a few that you might like to explore:
Campaign Monitor (Australia based)

JangoMail
Constant Contact
Get Response
AWeber

Did you know? According to Pew Internet, 94 per cent of adults who are online send and read emails and there are nearly three billion email accounts in the world—that's a lot of people to tap into!

How to create a great enewsletter:
Make it free. If you don't make content free in your enews, others will and you will give people less reason to subscribe and a reason to subscribe to your competitor.

Be sure to focus on your speciality or your industry and don't deviate too much. You need to appear as a specialist in your field as everyone who reads your enews is a potential customer/sale or a word of mouth advocate for your business.

Keep your design and formatting consistent with your website and your other promotional material—you want your audience to subconsciously link your enews with your other branding.

Format clearly and consistently. Outline each topic or paragraph with a clear heading followed by a subheading of important details, for example, price, date, or location followed by the body text of approximately one hundred words. Every topic should include a link and each enews should include at least three links back to your website interspersed throughout the content.

Use it as a pointer. The enews is a brilliant marketing tool to work in conjunction with your other tools. Point your enews subscribers towards a central point, ideally your website. If you don't have a website yet, point people to your blog or Facebook page, or a digital space where you store all your information about your services, products or events.

The first three items from the top are the most important and will be read the most. Make these three items what you want everyone to read as a priority such as events or important upcoming dates or anything that is a revenue making experience for you.

Make your enews regular and consistent. Send it out at exactly the same time and day on a regular basis. I recommend aiming for a monthly enews and send it out the morning of a weekday

Don't send them too often! The only clause to this rule is if your content is something that needs to be sent regularly (such as daily affirmations, which TUT do really well).

Do you know? 75% of people reported they would resent a brand after being bombarded by emails (Emailvision Survey, 2013).

Kept it short and readable and clean up your phrases. Make sure your articles and items are limited to short paragraphs and are readable. Use bullet points and graphics where possible. Use the paragraphs as a teaser and utilise the "read more" function to point people towards your website. The read more function is usually a button that can be found in the toolbar.

On average, medium sized content snippets (141 - 1,200 characters) generated 106% more "click through" activity than large snippets (larger than 1,200 characters), (Curata Curation Habits Report, 2012).

The main aim of your content should be to make people want more, whether that's more information, products or services— leave them a tiny bit curious so they'll read your site or contact you.

Keep your enews "non spammy"! You've see spam and you can easily get a sense of the cheapness of the words and how to avoid it.

Make sure your enews is professional. Stick to a more formal tone and avoid waffling about what you've been eating for breakfast or how you've been feeling. Consider this much like you would a hardcopy newsletter that you'd see at your child's school or via your neighbourhood watch (but much more interesting, of course!)

What to put in your enews
You may like to experiment with this formula:
30 per cent teasers: to other content, hints at what is coming up, grab a significant sentence or two from a blog post
50 per cent quality information: perhaps a short blog piece or content in full (200 – 400 words are plenty)
20 per cent direct promotion: products, services, sales etc.

Sporadically—every four to six months—make your enews purely about the readers, cut out the promotion and offer quality content and/or a free product or service or ask them a question to invite conversation.

Include a clear call to action. Make your readers do something. That could include going to your website, booking an appointment or providing you with feedback. Aim to have at least three calls to action per enews—even if they are the same.

Examples of what to include in your enews:
- events
- special offers, discounts and sales
- new services
- business updates
- a profile on a service or product (especially if you offer more than one) e.g. 'What is kinesiology'
- articles e.g. 'how can kinesiology help with fertility'
- personal updates
- lists (links of helpful websites, top five helpful hints lists)
- currently reading or inspirational books
- inspirational quotes (one or two per email is fine)
- affirmations
- staff news (new employees, babies, staff

leaving/retiring)
- business awards/nominations or any recognition
- staff profiles
- social photos
- cross promotional feature of a friend's/peer's business or service—ask that they do the same for you
- competition to win your service or product
- a client/customer testimonial or case study
- surveys
- free products—e.g. downloadable meditation, voucher, ebook etc
- question and answer interviews
- short video clip—perhaps introducing yourself or talking through a topic
- forecast—what is coming up for you, give your recipients a sneak peek

Make sure you set up your template so that every enews includes:
- contact details
- a pointer to websites (include several hyperlinks throughout the enews if necessary)
- a pointer to all social media platforms you're on (e.g. Facebook, Twitter, Instagram, YouTube, Blog etc)
- an unsubscribe option
- privacy policy/statement
- a forward to a friend option to make sure your readers' friends sign up too
- disclaimer—this can link to your disclaimer on your website
- copyright statement

Open rate
MailChimp has a handy inbuilt tool where you can check your statistics and see how many people have read your enews and which links they have clicked on.

If your open rate (the percentage of people that are actively opening your email) is more than twenty five per cent, you're doing well. Most industries (on average) don't have a higher open rate than thirty per cent. Some, such as, IT, fashion, events, education and legal, barely make it past twenty per cent. So if you're consistently hitting percentages up in the forties, fifties or sixties and you have a decent amount of people subscribed to your list, then you are doing an exemplary job and at least double the industry average.

If you're not reaching at least twenty per cent (even if you have an enormous mailing list) then something is askew and it is most likely your content. Once you've perfected your content, then you can work on creating a snazzy subject line.

Remember: according to MailChimp's research following the pattern of an average workday, most emails are opened between 9am and 12pm, with 1pm to 5pm coming in just behind. After 9pm, open rates make a steep decline.

Subject line

The subject line is the first thing that people will see when it hits their inbox. Crafting the perfect subject line is an art form, a rewarding one, which can entice people to open the email and read the content. Try and think of an appealing subject line that people will want to click on.

Here is a list of the worst performing subject lines according to MailChimp's research.

1. Last Minute Gift—We Have The Answer
2. Valentines—Shop Early & Save 10%
3. Give a Gift Certificate this Holiday
4. Valentine's Day Salon and Spa Specials!
5. Gift Certificates—Easy & Elegant Giving—Let Them Choose
6. Need More Advertising Value From Your Marketing Partner?
7. [COMPANYNAME] Pioneers in Banana Technology
8. Renewal
9. [COMPANYNAME] Holiday Sales Event
10. The Future of International Trade

11. [COMPANYNAME] for your next dream home.

Here are some examples of really successful subject lines that MailChimp have collated:
1. [COMPANYNAME] Staff Shirts & Photos
2. [COMPANYNAME] and [COMPANYNAME] Invites You!
3. ATTENTION [COMPANYNAME] Staff!
4. Invitation from [COMPANYNAME]
5. We're Throwing a Party
6. October 2005 Newsletter

Subscribers
Subscribers are the people that sign up to receive your enews. This list of names and email addresses is practically invaluable and building it should form part of your marketing strategy. This database is more important than your social media followers because they are more likely to purchase something from you.

Microsoft Excel is a user friendly program to use to collate your database of subscribers but if you have many subscribers or would like something more complex with more features you may want to investigate CRM programs such as Highrise, Mind Body, Namaste Light or Zen Planner.

It is vital that you invest time into developing your database of subscribers.

Developing your subscriber database
One of the best ways to ensure people sign up is to make signing up as easy as possible. People shouldn't have to search for where your sign up form is. It should be prominently placed on your website, Facebook page and other social media platforms.

Here are some handy tricks to increase your enews subscribers:
- Offer something for free
- Give them something
- Put a link to sign up in your Twitter biography
- If you work from physical premises, have a sign-up

sheet at your front desk or reception area.

- Hold a stall at your local markets or promotional fair. Have a sign-up sheet at your stall or a flyer that people can take away with them to sign up later.
- Make sure you are sending out content that people actually want to read
- Offer to give short community talks or lead workshops for free and then explain that people can sign up to your enews should they want to learn more about you and what you offer.
- Tweet regularly with a link to sign up to your enews
- Ask people over the phone or in person 'have you signed up to my enews yet?'
- Include a link in your email signature, 'be sure to sign up to my enews…'
- Incorporate a sign-up widget on your Facebook page, blog and website. MailChimp, Facebook and WordPress all have relatively easy functions to do this.
- Run a competition. An example is, 'the first five people to sign up to our enews will receive a free massage' (or something you can offer that is of low cost to you). MailChimp is very handy for this as it can tell you the exact time someone has signed up to the list. Announce this competition via your social media platforms.
- Any time you host an event or workshop, ensure you have a sign-up sheet where people can easily write down their name and email address.
- Ensure every client, upon their initial consultation/visit fills out a form providing their contact details and a tick to subscribe to your enews option
- In addition to a static enews sign-up form, why not have a pop up sign up so that every time a new user goes to your website, a box flashes up and prompts them to join. A good example can be found at www.marketingprofs.com
- Remind your social media followers that an enews is pending and that they should sign up now! Make sure you include the link to where they can sign up—make it as easy as possible for them.

- Make sure that your enews template has a 'forward to friend' option. Anything you can do to make your readers' lives easier and your content easily shareable will be rewarded with more readers and viewers.
- When promoting your enews detail the benefits and why people should sign up. For example, do you offer special subscriber only discounts?

'[Consumers] tend to be seeking tangible incentives like discounts or coupons. However not many businesses are offering these – only a quarter of SMEs and 30% of large businesses – which could be a missed opportunity,' Sensis Social Media Report, May 2015.

Examples of what you can offer for free for everyone who signs up:
- downloadable meditation
- unlimited access to restricted parts of your website
- templates
- audio recording
- short ebook
- personalised message/astrology reading/numerology chart
- fact sheet on your area of expertise
- mandala
- prize
- discount voucher to your service
- intuitive reading
- free advertising
- coffee date (be prepared for what this promise could instigate!)
- YouTube clip or video restricted to enews subscribers only
- a special recipe.

Activity: you didn't think I'd let you get away with not setting an intention for your enews now, did you? Stop what you are doing right now and write down your enews goal. Your written goal statement should look like this:

By [date], I will have [number] people subscribed to my enews list and each enews will have an open rate of [percentage] or higher. I encourage you to revise this statement monthly or quarterly.

Activity: if you already have a regular enews going out, list three things of value that your readers are getting with each edition. Be specific. For example, a subscriber only discount, priority access to tickets for a workshop and event dates all in one handy spot (even better if you can make this downloadable or printable). If you fail to come up with three, you have just identified what area you need to work on with your enews content.

If you haven't started your enews yet, you can still list the three things that you want your readers to get out of your enews. Keep this list as part of your marketing plan, so you can refer back to every time you compose your enews.

Activity: reach out to clients/customers that you haven't seen for awhile. If you have a client management system you will be able to pull a list of clients you haven't seen for 12-24 months and send them an email to reconnect with them. Perhaps offering them a discount voucher for their next appointment will bring them back into your realm. I'm not enforcing this as mandatory practise because quite often clients leave our lives for Divine reasons, for the highest good of themselves and yourself.

Legalities

Until September 2014, users had to sign up to an enews or mailing list and then confirm via an email link in accordance with privacy laws. This was known as a double opt in sign up method. Now, you can have a single opt in system, which is much easier to get subscribers, particularly all the lazier ones (myself included… that extra click just seems like too much work some days!)

You cannot data share, especially with the brand new privacy law in place. This means you cannot give your database list to anyone. What you can do, however, is partner with someone and organise an exchange. You could organise to profile a peer and their offerings in your enews with an understanding they will profile you in their enews. Keep in mind that you will want to organise this exchange with someone with a database that benefits and complements your business.

Do you know? It is illegal to sign up someone to your enews list without their permission—they must do so themselves.

You can also purchase lists of contacts to add to your database. But wouldn't you rather have people sign up of their own accord? What sounds better? Two thousand email addresses that may not belong to real people and even they are real they may never be interested in your service or product? Or would you prefer a database of two hundred real people that have an interest in your industry that could easily translate into a sale?

Safe list
Include a sign up or welcome email that encourages your new subscribers to include your address on their safe list or adds it to their electronic address book. This will ensure you don't get shipped into their junk folder and they miss your important messages.

Most email programs provide the option to set up auto responders. These are scheduled enews to automatically be sent out at designated intervals. You might have one set up to go out when a person subscribes, welcoming them to your service. This is great if you have content that is not time dependant or you are running an online course etc. You can just schedule one enews to go out per week, and so your subscribers can be at different stages of their relationship with you and your enews.

Tip: keep a folder (hardcopy, inbox or on your computer) and label it "enews". Chuck into this folder anything that can be used at some point for your enews—quotes, pictures, rambling thoughts, links to blog posts etc. Any time you have an event, workshop, discount, new service, business addition—be sure to make a note of it in this folder. That will make it easier to come back to when it's time to do your enews.

After the enews
Don't assume that once your enews has been sent out that its job has been done. Set up an automated system (also known as an auto responder) so that anyone who signs up automatically receives a copy of the most recent one. .

MailChimp will also provide you with a shortened link to your enews once it has been sent. Please make great use of this link by posting it to your social media platforms and reminding people if they missed the latest edition of the enews that they can view it by clicking on the link.
Remember: it's not just enough to get people to sign up but it's also vital to get people to read what you have written as well. Everybody's time is incredibly precious, as you would know. Make it worth their while.

Auto responders
MailChimp is pretty clever. You can schedule it to send automated emails on your behalf, send people a welcome email when they sign up to your enews and send out scheduled emails. You can personalise emails according to what people like, what they look at on the internet and provide recommendations that are targeted towards your subscribers after they have purchased a particular product or service. Sounds a bit stalky, right? Not really, retail and other industries have been doing it for years based on what you prefer. It's not really that much different than a doctor keeping a file on you.

Facebook is the most used social media platform in the world. Fourteen million Australians use Facebook (as at 1 September, 2015).

Facebook is a phenomenal promotional tool. You can post links, images, photos, paragraphs, short statuses and events—most things work on this digital platform. It is, however, an ever changing beast, so it's important you are proactive in relearning its changes to make the most of its promotional power.

It would be futile to deeply go into the advantages and disadvantages of Facebook because as a business, you should really be taking advantage of it. Your competitors are probably already in this space and your clients/customers definitely are.

People over 65 years are starting to join and use Facebook more than ever, so be sure to factor that into your marketing ideals and target demographic. Teenagers and young adults tend not to use Facebook as much anymore, it is "old hat" for them, so explore other methods of communicating with them unless their decision maker for your product/service is their parent, teacher, caregiver or another key adult in their life.

Before you start
1. Have a selection of images ready, including your logo, business photos, pictures to accompany your initial posts and a Facebook page banner. Your Facebook page banner will need to be at least 400 pixels wide. The best size to fit the banner, if you are designing a custom image is 851 x 315 pixels.
2. Have your website, blog or contact details ready to go.
3. Write a couple of posts or statuses so you can schedule them in.

Setting up a Facebook business page
You will need a personal Facebook account to set up a Facebook business page. You can have multiple business pages from the

one user and likewise, you can have multiple people in control of the business page, should you choose. These people are called "admins".

1. Go to the top right hand corner of your Facebook screen.
2. Click the small cog shaped icon.
3. Click "Create Page".

Customising your Facebook page
On your Facebook page you can customise your tabs so you can prioritise what your audience views. If you have a lot of events, you may want to consider placing this as a priority or maybe you want to show off your YouTube channel more?

Settings > more > manage tabs >
From there you can reorder, to put the most important thing first (I recommend About section, with Timeline fixed as the first tab).
After your About tab, I recommend your enews signup tab, linked to your MailChimp account (or enews platform). Here are some explanations of how to do so:
http://kb.mailchimp.com/integrations/facebook/add-a-signup-form-to-your-facebook-page

Did you know? You can create your own tabs. This is handy if you want to use coupons, run contests or want a video or image tab.

Here are some low cost or free places that help you customise and create your tabs:
- Pagemondo
- Shortstack
- Woobox
- TabSite

Facebook's algorithm
Be aware that not all your posts will automatically reach all of your community. Much like Google, Facebook utilises a user based algorithm, which changes regularly. It's vital that you

have relevant and engaging content that will actively encourage your "likers" to search out your page and content. Facebook keeps an eye on everyone's using behaviour, so it guesses which pages, posts and items you want to see the most based on your past behaviour. The more often you visit a Facebook page, them more prominent it will be in your timeline. Our aim is to keep our audience engaged with our page, so it's not getting hidden in the noise of Facebook. It's often the last fifty pages you have viewed (as a user).

How do you do that? As at the time of writing this book, Facebook favours organic videos the most, meaning that organic videos (not ones via an external link such as YouTube etc) will reach more audience. However, to consistently reach an audience, you need to provide a variety of posts and formats the algorithm also favours variety. No matter what the algorithm is favouring, there is one golden rule to ensure maximum organic reach just provide great, engaging content.

Do you know? There's little numbers at the base of your post that will tell you how many people have sighted your post.

How to get people interested in your Facebook page/more likes
- advertising (on Facebook and externally)
- encourage engagement
- encourage sharing of your posts
- undertake a competition
- promote your Facebook page everywhere you can think of: blog, website, other social media platforms, enews, hard copy newsletter, physical premises, email signatures or even your car door!
- Above all, be sure to have great content that will entice people to seek you out.

Here are some content ideas of for Facebook:
- links to your blog post (this works well when accompanied by a "pull quote" and an image from your piece)

- audience questions—inviting opinion, asking for advice, suggestions (avoid yes or no questions)
- your location (for example, 'I'm currently enjoying a tai chi class in the park' coupled with an image)
- a picture or photo
- links to an interesting article or blog posts (particularly your own)
- a reminder of your services, products and events
- funny anecdotes
- polls
- testimonials or successes of a client/customer
- memes and pictures (keep it tasteful and non offensive)
- business or relevant personal milestones
- facts or statistics
- useful resources
- inspirational quotes (in written or image form) from other people or create your own
- your own opinions (if they are gregarious, expect to invite conversation)
- promotional offers
- share links of like-minded community events/businesses/services
- latest industry news, findings, reports, articles, research—particularly if this supports your modality.
- countdowns to events/workshops or special holidays
- "business brags", for example, you could brag about the three new clients you signed up this week or the satisfaction you have felt after a particular client or session
- share a favourite book or movie and why you like it. Remember to invite discussion.
- any new positive change in the business
- link up your other platforms. For example, let people know how to find you on Twitter, Instagram, LinkedIn, YouTube etc.
- share images that link back to your branding (for example, Starbucks share images of sunshine and warmth to complement their branding)

- post a quote, article or statistic from an expert
- TBT stands for "throw back Thursday"; where on Thursday you can rehash something from the past. This is a great idea if you want to reflect on how far you have come in twelve months or want to revisit a post that has been popular in the past.
- "share" other people's content
- post a "thank you" post
- information, pages or images from your website
- use relevant holidays—share a celebratory or reflective post
- special offers (see below)
- competitions (see below)
- photos from a networking or industry event (try to upload these as soon as possible. The next day is ideal).
- invite people to sign up to your enews
- share breaking or important industry related news
- profile a client, employee or co-worker
- create a special only for Facebook using a promo or whisper code (see below)

Don't forget: to respond to comments and ask and answer questions, making Facebook a conversational tool.

Writing for Facebook
An easy assumption to make is that you can write with reckless abandon on Facebook and that not every post counts. Just because the content isn't static and is forever moving, does not mean that you do not apply the same copywriting techniques that you would for any other marketing activity.

Here are some tips on crafting great Facebook statuses:
1. Don't waffle on! Keep your status to a maximum of three short sentences. Save lengthy pieces for your blog or website.
2. Use correct grammar and spelling to convey a professional tone and generate trust from your audience.
3. Don't overuse grammar! If you're using more than one ellipses or exclamation mark, you're doing it wrong! If

everything you say is an EXCLAMATION then your real announcements will get lost in the noise.

4. Before you post, think about how you can refine the same message into a sentence or two. (This is why Twitter is great because you have to limit what you're saying to 140 characters or less).

5. Don't forget to make your audience do something. That could include commenting, visiting your blog or website, phoning for an appointment, pondering something or praying. Limit statuses that are purely statements.

Did you know? Manners cost nothing but double everything! Including the word please in your call-to-action can increase your engagement by almost double, according to *The Most Effective Calls to Action for Facebook Posts*, by Ayaz Nanji, 18 June 2014.

Offers

Facebook is one of the greatest cost free ways to communicate when you have offers. Here are some tips on how to maximise how you share your offer:

1. Make a negative claim before stating the positive offer. This will create a reaction or response and the positive offer, in contrast, will be much more appealing than if you were to just write the offer.

2. For example, 'it's really cold outside, so here's a discount to warm you up.'

3. Explain your offer. Be transparent otherwise people assume it's too good to be true—but not cringe worthy. A poor example would be 'I not getting much interest in XX service, so I'm going to drop the price because I really believe that you will benefit from this.'

4. Offer something of value.

5. Offer something that will require someone to make a purchase. Try not to give away too many freebies without the customers having to do something in return, either purchase another product, sign up to your enews or attend a seminar.

6. An offer will be more effective in the long run if you

encourage more people through the "door". For example, a two for one offer is better for your client base and potential sales than offering fifty per cent off for one customer.

Promotional codes
Promotional codes sometimes known as "whisper" codes can be shared via social media only, so that your dedicated social media followers can use them when they purchase a product or service. If you have an online store, they can use them as a discount coupon when they reach the shopping cart stage or you can encourage them to use the whisper codes at your physical premises or when booking via the phone. This will reinforce that social proof that we discuss more later and those who aren't following you on Facebook will want to so they don't miss out on future promotions.
I like to use whisper code words that also have a high vibration such as "success", "abundance", "beautiful" and so forth.

Competitions
To date, Facebook has changed its terms and conditions on competitions several times. It's worth keeping an eye on these changes to ensure you don't get banned from Facebook. www.facebook.com/legal/terms
As at March 2015, the terms state that you cannot ask anyone to do anything that involves their personal page. That means you cannot ask them to share a post or tag someone to win. However, they can comment on or like a post and be chosen at random. Commenting and liking a post still are beneficial and are worth factoring into your marketing plan. Your readers' Facebook friends will see the comment or like and it may also encourage them to do so, increasing your audience even further. You can choose a winner at random the "old fashioned" way by collecting the names and pulling them out of a hat or you can use an online generator. Do an internet search for a list of winner generators and cut and paste your competition participants from Facebook and the generator will take care of picking a winner for you!
Avoid the words: coupon, sweepstakes, contest and promotion when running a social media competition. Instead use winner,

win, winning, lucky, events, free, bonus… you get the idea. People don't want to know the process—they just want to know the end result for them, or at least the possible end result.

Remember: ensure that your competition is working for you and you're not just running one for the sake of it. Ask yourself, what will this competition do for my business? Make sure your answer includes something tangible, such as signing up more subscribers, getting more interest in your Facebook page etc.

Competition ideas:
- caption this image
- comment below with your (something relevant the competition)
- comment with your name
- post your own pictures in the comments.

Competition prize ideas:
- free treatment/service/product
- free promotion of their business/service page
- buy something nice to giveaway
- discount voucher
- second hand or CDs that you want to give away?
- get a business to donate a prize in lieu of promotion
- choose a group of winners and offer them VIP access to your blog (set up a few 'password protected' posts and grant the winners the password.

Tip: the more valuable the prize, the more likely people will be to enter.

Cover Photo
You may like to alternate your Facebook cover photo (the header image) as part of your social media marketing campaign. I recommend changing it a maximum of once every three months and ensure that it's consistently connected to your branding/logo. You may, however, like to jazz up your cover image to coincide with a major event or holiday that is pertinent to your business or

to promote your latest discount or offer. But if no one can see your logo or instantly recognise your branding when looking at your Facebook landing page, then you're doing your page a disservice.

Advertising

I have found Facebook advertising to be beneficial, especially as it's relatively inexpensive.

Initially, there was some scepticism of its validity but if you target your audience appropriately, it should prove to be an effective advertising tool for your business.

Facebook advertising will give you options to choose which demographic you want to target when creating your campaign. Selecting Australia (if that's the country you operate from) will help to eliminate fake accounts. If you operate a service that is location specific, you can also limit it to that city. There's no point having someone from Switzerland liking your page or post if you only offer in-person services in Brisbane.

You can advertise your business to get more "likes" or you can promote certain posts or do both. Initially, I would suggest promoting your business page and then once you have acquired more than a thousand "likes" focus on promoting special events, sales, services or promotions that you have.

Don't spend your entire advertising dollar unless you believe you'll recoup it. Meaning, if you want to promote a certain post about your products or services, you might have a hunch that you'll get one new client out of it. Let's err on the side of prudence and say that that client only purchases $60 worth of product or service. You now have a maximum spend for that advertising campaign, knowing that you'll at least break even. There is a tiny bit of guess work initially, until you have trialled Facebook advertising a few times to see what results it brings. You'll know that a client has come to you after seeing a Facebook post because you'll have remembered to collect data when they initially contact you or attend one of your sessions (right?).

Tip: to make sure that your advertisement is getting seen by the relevant people, choose the applicable demographic that you established in the chapter about **Identifying your target demographics**.

If you just want to promote a certain post on your business page, click "boost" in the bottom right hand corner of the post and choose your options. If you want to promote your business page, click on your page, click "build audience" and then you can choose from a few options, including Promote Website, Promote Page or Use Ads Manager.

You can find all about Facebook advertising by visiting www.facebook.com/advertising. You'll need a credit card, so have that ready.

Twitter and Instagram operate under a similar advertising model. I recommend dipping your toe into the advertising waters via Facebook and cross promoting rather than spending hundreds or thousands of dollars advertising on all three platforms at once.

According to the Sensis Social Media Report for 2015, 69% of businesses who have used Facebook advertising believe that it was effective.

Remember: before you start any Facebook advertising, be clear what your annual advertising budget is and don't blow it all at once!

Discussion groups

Facebook discussion groups are often a concentrated group of people talking about a really specific topic. This can be a really useful way of reaching out to a group of people that are already interested in the type of services you offer.

Whatever the topic, there is probably already a discussion group in existence, which is great! There's a potential audience just waiting for you. However, there are some important things to remember—do not become spammy or pushy. Discussion groups are an online conversation, so feel free to offer your advice or opinion or share useful links, clips or resources or recommend books etc. Don't push your services at any chance you get, this is just an opportunity to share your knowledge, be part of a discussion and gain some credibility with like-minded individuals. You may sporadically promote your business, if it's in relation to the topic being discussed, but use your intuition and humbleness as a delicate way to approach this, just like you would if it were a real-life discussion. Make sure you learn and abide by the group rules—otherwise you may be asked to leave.

Tip: be sure to familiarise yourself with the group's terms and conditions. The administrator of the group may have specified that there's to be no promotion.

You may also like to offer this group something special— perhaps if you're testing out a new product or service, this might be your confidant or beta testing group—your trusted like-minded peers. Offer them something for free in exchange for their honest feedback.

Why not start your own discussion group? You will have to set the parameters for group behaviours and invite and lead discussions, most of the time. Once the group gains momentum, your role could then just be to moderate.

Facebook has a terrific starter guide for people beginning their own discussion groups:
https://www.facebook.com/groupadmins/tips.pdf/

Statistics
Facebook has its own statistics tool for business pages which will tell you immediately how many people each post has reached. You'll find this located in the bottom left hand corner of each post or under the "Insights" tab of your admin panel. Facebook has a complicated algorithm that works out who sees your posts and who doesn't. It's not just assumed that everyone that has "liked" your page gets to see them in your newsfeed. People are more likely to see your posts pop up in their timeline

if they engage with you frequently, so your best bet is to ensure you are working on content that invites them to engage.

Why is it important to have statistics?
The information that you can garner is very useful so you can identify your strengths and weaknesses and the areas where you need to improve. Perhaps you are getting a lot of page views but not many sales? If so, maybe you need to work on your sales pitch? It's clear you're getting a lot of people on your site but something isn't quite making them buy. Time to jazz up the pictures, lower the price or reword your text.

Twitter

Twitter is a fast-paced social networking and information platform that is considered micro blogging. It's growing at a rate of more than 25 per cent users per year. So really, what are you waiting for?

Twitter is, perhaps, my favourite medium. I love the active yet succinct conversational aspect of it. I have found that it encourages people to be extra creative to get their message across, as there is a limit of 140 characters per tweet (a short message). Tweets have a very short life span—generally up to a few minutes, maybe more if you're lucky. So the content really does have to be timely and engaging in order to catch someone's attention.

It's also really portable—you can add it to your smart phone or tablet and tweet when you are on the go or out at an event. It differs from Facebook in that it has a shorter shelf life, so you can tweet more often with less information. Facebook is slightly more static in that you will want to reduce your posts to a couple per day.

Once you have created a Twitter account, you can post tweets that anyone can read and reply to. The exception is that you can choose to have your account set on private and only people who "follow" you can see what you tweet. Your followers will see your tweets displayed in their timeline. A timeline is a column of live tweets from everyone you follow (or what they have "retweeted").

You can have as many Twitter accounts as you would like and they can all be easily accessed from your smart phone.

Getting started
Twitter has such a good 'getting started guide' that there is no point me reinventing the wheel. Visit this page:
https://support.twitter.com/articles/215585-getting-started-with-twitter#

Here are some other places to get started:
https://business.twitter.com/start-tweeting
Log into www.twitter.com

Twitter terms
Here are some basic terms to get you familiar with Twitter.

Retweet
A retweet [RT] is when you share someone else's tweet. There is a special function in Twitter that makes this effortlessly possible.

A RT is like a little magic gift from the Twitter Gods. A person may retweet you which means all their followers will see your tweet and know that you exist. Essentially, if someone retweets you, they are saying 'hey, take a look at this' (hopefully for the right reasons). If people like what you are saying, find your information useful and topical, they may retweet you.

Retweet others. Remember that retweeting is saying to your followers 'hey, look at this', so only retweet things that you want your followers to look at and that mildly associate with you.

Tip: the best time for getting retweets is generally very late evening.

Tweets containing images garner more interest and retweets than not (some statistics even suggest up to fifty per cent more!) Now Twitter has a multiple image upload option, so you can display many images in the one tweet. Uploading your images straight to Twitter will increase their chances of a retweet or getting noticed as opposed to linking via Instagram, Twitpic or Facebook.

Followers
Like Facebook, you want to increase your followers (known as 'likers' on Facebook) because the more people that sight your message, the wider your potential sales group is going to be. The people that you follow will also have valuable information, share interesting links to articles, blogs and websites and hold

entertaining and stimulating conversations. The best part? You don't even have to leave your bed!

Tip: follow people that you want to follow you back.

Handle
A handle is your username. It's the name that sits at the end of the "@" symbol that people will identify and interact with and search for you with. It is all one word and can contain numerals, letters and the underscore symbol.

Choose a handle that relates to your business and that people will automatically know is associated with your business. For example, if your business name is Spirit Heaven, see if the handle @spiritheaven is available. (It's not—I've checked). You may have to come up with a few closely-related alternatives:
Spirheaven
Spirit_heaven
Spiritheaven_Adelaide

Hashtag
A hashtag is a noun for a topic talked about on social media— particularly utilised by Twitter—that is preceded by a hashtag symbol to make it searchable within the social media platform. It's a quick way of finding other users that are interacting about the same topic. It's more than forgivable to let proper grammar and spelling go for the sake of a good hashtag.
To make your hashtag effective keep it as short as possible, which may mean using abbreviations, skipping some words or not using spaces. Do a quick hashtag search before using one to see that you are keeping it consistent with others.

Tip: keep the hashtag readable, succinct and clear.

Here are some hashtags that will help you connect with your desired community that you can use intermittently throughout your tweets:
- your city e.g., #sydney
- your services/products e.g. #massage #healing #yoga

- people e.g. #rumi #ellendegeneres
- your events e.g. #spiritday #psychicexpo
- regular Twitter favourites e.g. #ff #askTwitter
- activities e.g. #amwriting
- campaigns e.g. #icebucketchallenge

Remember: don't be hasty and jump onto a hashtag that has absolutely no relevance to your tweet. You'll just look silly and lose respect.

A trending hashtag will generally have a lifespan of about twenty four hours this relates to current affairs and hot topic news or entertainment items, whereas locations and activities have an ongoing presence.

Trending topics
Twitter collates a list of topics that are talked about the most on Twitter.
Think the trending topic doesn't apply to you? Think creatively! Maybe the topic is Ellen DeGeneres. Why not do your research and tweet this:
Did you know that @EllenDegeneres gets four #massages a week?

Sure, I just completely made that up but with a little bit of a Google search you could find some relevant facts that will enable you to jump on the trending topic bandwagon, making you a part of the biggest conversation in the world, thus making you more noticeable and searchable.

Trends Map <http://trendsmap.com/> will show you a map of where you are and what is trending, using a word cloud (the bigger the word, the more it is trending).

Direct messages
A direct message (or DM) is otherwise known as a private tweet, between someone you follow and who also follows you. Auto DMs look amateur and "spammy". I suggest giving auto DMs the flick and engaging people in conversation instead.

Twitter bio
Include a succinct bio on your Twitter profile. Don't leave it blank and keep people guessing. Use key words and utilise (but don't overuse) the hashtag function. Include industry relevant keywords, such as blogging, yoga, dietician etc.

Putting a location is important, particularly if a lot of your business is in person. List all your websites and what you do there.

Here's an example of one of my Twitter bios:

Jones the Writer
@jones_writer
Freelance copy/creative writer at jonesthewriter.com, yoga instructor, Marketing Manager .Also, incenseandhappiness.com
Adelaide

Image
Make sure you put an image as your avatar. Don't leave it as the default "egg"; people will assume that you are a "spambot". Show them you are a real person and someone to connect to. Make your headshot clear and visible. People love to know who they are conversing with. A happy headshot or logo is ideal.
In your header picture (the wider one that sits behind your profile picture) you can include a picture of your logo, a product or one of your images. Remember to keep your branding (your look and feel) consistent.

Tip: don't be fooled by the seemingly impersonal approach that social media offers, I have met a lot of fantastic people on Twitter—friends, boyfriends and have gleaned several clients this way.

Tweet structure
Your very brief sentence goes first, followed by any relevant links (you can use a service called Bitly to shorten website links for aesthetic and space saving reasons) and then leave relevant

hashtags until the end of the tweet.

Tip: if you're linking to an external page such as your website, blog or Facebook ensure you have a sentence that entices readers to click!

The Twitter audience is more forgivable than Facebook in the frequency of posts. It's still important to invite conversation and provide interesting content however.

Here are some ideas of what your tweets could contain:
- links to your blog post
- audience questions—invite opinion, asking for advice, suggestions (avoid yes or no questions)
- your location (e.g. I'm currently enjoying a tai chi class in the park)
- a picture or photo
- links to an interesting article or blog post (particularly your own)
- a reminder of your services/products
- funny anecdotes
- memes and pictures (these have a good share rate on Twitter)
- quick facts or statistics
- inspirational quotes (apparently these are the most retweeted things on Twitter)
- your own opinions (if they are gregarious, expect to invite conversation)
- promotional offers
- tweet interesting stuff
- share links of like-minded community events/businesses/services
- tips from your speciality area (see below)
- latest industry news, findings, reports, articles, research—particularly if this supports your modality
- countdowns to events/workshops or special holidays
- business related positives, e.g. three new clients this week or your satisfaction after a particular session

- testimonials from clients
- choose five people you follow (for the week) and start a conversation about something in their bio or website. For example, 'does Edinburgh still have that amazing taco shop?' (be aware that extensive conversations excluding others will bore your followers, clog up their timeline and potentially get you unfollowed)
- people you recommend such as your own healers, therapists, health professionals, fitness classes, suppliers etc
- tell an anecdote or story over a few consecutive tweets (use this technique sparingly)
- write a Haiku
- goals or future visions
- tweet about Twitter—for some reason; people love to talk about Twitter on Twitter!
- your most retweeted or favourite tweet of the year
- ask your followers for social media advice!
- how can you make your Twitter followers' lives better? What advice or solution can you offer in an instant?

Top tips on Twitter!
Here's a great way to encourage conversation on Twitter and keep your followers engaged and interested.
Make a list of ten tips in an area of your speciality and choose a day to sporadically tweet these tips. Your tips might include helpful insights for the physical body and how to heal it, natural remedies, and reminders about getting outside or eating vegetables, anatomical knowledge, ancient philosophy or anything that your business specialises in.
You may even like to create a hashtag, e.g. #tuesdaytips or #yogatips #candlemakingtips

Tip: use a scheduler such as Hootsuite so you don't have to worry about getting onto Twitter every hour or so.

Be sure to alert people that you are doing it. That means letting people know the day before on Facebook, in person or perhaps by sending a group email or text message, so they can join in the fun!

Remember: what may be common knowledge to you may be a beautiful, new and life changing insight for someone else.

Things to remember
Add some personality to your tweets. Think of Twitter as a dinner with a big group of people and you're all having a chat. What would you want to talk about at the dinner? Be human in your approach but remain professional. Once you spend some time on Twitter, you will pick up the general feel from reading others' tweets. Talk to your followers or potential followers about their interests too—don't just keep the conversation one sided.

Once your Twitter account starts to grow, you will (hopefully) be getting a lot of replies (also known as @ replies). You don't necessarily have to respond to each and every one, especially as this will get boring in other people's timelines and you run the risk of them unfollowing you.

If people do unfollow you, don't take it personally (unless you're losing a thousand followers a day, then you might be doing something quite wrong).

You can learn so much from other people. Do your research and spend time watching what successful Twitterers do—how they talk, interact, the frequency of their tweets etc. Make a Twitter list of people you admire—remember the lists name' is public, so make it something complimentary like 'great tweeters' as opposed to something creepy like 'people I watch'.
Engage these people in conversation (a couple of replies to their tweets are enough, don't hound them every day).

Tips:
1. Don't retweet all mentions you get, do so sparingly.
2. Never ask someone to retweet you, it's bad etiquette.
3. Create lists of influential tweeters to keep abreast of their content and engage in conversation where relevant and

fitting.

Remember: Twitter is an arm of your customer service, treat it that way. Respond to a tweet (particularly if it's critical) within an hour—most people expect this—particularly if you are a larger business.

Twitter advertising
You want quality followers that are going to interact with you, which ultimately lead to a purchase from you. You can't do this if you are just followed by thousands of "spambots".

Join in or start a conversation. Chat Salad (chatsalad.com) lists upcoming pre-scheduled chats by time and hashtag. Remember to think outside the box and chat with potential clients, as well as industry peers.

Instagram

Instagram, which launched in October 2010, is another ever increasing platform that has a healthy 300 million users (this has doubled since 2013), with more than 75 million people using it daily. At January 2015, 51 per cent of users were male and 49 per cent were female. It's a visual app where you can upload photos and images which users can 'like' and comment on.

Australians are using Instagram an average of twenty six times each week. The biggest user group is aged between 18 and 29 years old. People spend just under ten minutes on Instagram, so you have to make sure your posts are eye catching.

It has recently introduced paid advertising to promote posts and flood them in other people's feed or timeline, even if not followed but many people have found success through Instagram and have become what is colloquially known as "Insta-famous", without having to do so.

The advantages of using Instagram are that it:
- is a great visual aid
- reaches a slightly different audience than Twitter and Facebook
- can link to Facebook (Facebook now own Instagram), Twitter, Flickr and other social media accounts, which is a great way of efficiently providing content
- is fun
- has built-in filters and photo effects to enhance your pictures
- can be great for hashtag competitions
- has a lot of celebrity users
- is mainly used by a younger demographic.

The downsides of using Instagram are that:
- it's mainly a visual medium, so it's rare that you will get to provide a lot of text

a wider audience don't get to reach you as easily as on Facebook and Twitter
it's not ideal as a standalone, it works best in conjunction with other platforms,
the use of hashtags are paramount with Instagram

- it's predominantly a mobile phone app so you will need a smart phone to use
- if you offer a service which doesn't have a lot of visual aspects, it can be hard to come up with content
- you can't hyperlink, meaning that people will have to manually type in your URL, which greatly reduces the chance of them doing so.

Tips:
1. Post one to two photos per day.
2. Include relevant hashtags.
3. Make sure there is a clear link back to your website. If you are posting a photo or image that you own, make sure there is a watermark with your website URL, logo, name or that it's mentioned in the caption section.

Content ideas:
- products
- making of products
- clients
- studio/business base
- behind the scenes of something significant
- something that reveals a secret
- inspirational quotes and sayings
- infographics
- artwork which is inspiring (remember your copyright obligations)
- chakras, yantras, mandalas, deities—anything that is linked to the service you offer
- before and after shots—you can use a collage app to help you
- anything that invokes feelings of warmth and love

- photos of yourself enjoying industry related lifestyle activities (e.g. getting a massage, doing yoga, hiking, enjoying a smoothie)
- artistic photos
- follow other people on Instagram to garner ideas and inspiration
- visual technique tips, for example, cooking, massage, physiotherapy, asana etc.

Did you know? The brand Old Spice (yes, THAT Old Spice) created a Choose Your Own Adventure narrative on Instagram by utilising tags and hashtags. A very fun way to pass an afternoon!

Flipagram

Flipagram is a great smart phone app that takes your photos or short clips and turns them into a funky video (a 'flipagram' complete with music) that you can social share easily. A Flipagram is ideal for Instagram, which automatically loads video content in a user's feed. You can also share your Flipagram via Facebook (and other platforms), remembering that Facebook's algorithm responds favourably to organic video content.

> 'We are visual creatures. When you doodle an image that captures the essence of an idea, you not only remember it, but you also help other people understand and act on it - which is generally the point of meetings in the first place,'
> Tom Wujec.

YouTube

YouTube is an online video streaming mechanism that anyone can access as long as they have access to the internet. It has over one billion users and approximately 12.4 million people streaming videos annually in Australia.

In 2011, E-commerce stacksandstacks.com—one of the Internet Retailer's Top 500—reported that a customer was 144 per cent more likely to make a purchase on something after seeing a video on it.

http://www.internetretailer.com/2011/03/07/product-videos-raise-purchase-likelihood-stacks-and-stacks

Another internet product company, Living Direct, had noticed an increase of 9 per cent more time spent on their webpages that contain video content by viewers. (October 2010)http://www.internetretailer.com/2010/10/07/living-direct-raises-conversions-video-demos

Tip: create a YouTube channel so you can upload all your clips (videos) into the one spot. Keep your channel consistent with your branding.

The advantages of using YouTube are that:
- it's a visual medium
- various studies have shown that 60 - 70 per cent of people prefer to watch a video over reading text
- it's free for users and viewers
- it makes your business more searchable
- it's low cost to produce a video
- it has an instant connection to your client or customer, rather than just disembodied voice/text like other mediums
- it is easy to share, distribute and refer back to, especially on other social media platforms
- it can present lots of information in a short amount of time
- it's great for demonstrating processes that require a

visual medium, such as yoga, EFT, massage techniques, art work, music etc
- like websites, YouTube is important for SEO, particularly as it is owned by Google
- it's particularly useful for selling products that wouldn't normally sell based on images alone.

Did you know? 85 per cent of adults around the world are regular YouTube visitors?

It need not be as complex as you might imagine. Most laptops, tablets and smart phones now have a decent inbuilt video camera, so it is unlikely that you'll need to buy, borrow or hire one, making it a cost effective way of promoting your products or services. You can even directly upload the video to YouTube from any of these items. If you want to edit it slightly, YouTube has a fairly straight forward video editor that you can use. You can find it here: www.youtube.com/editor

Tips on making a great YouTube video:
1. Choose excellent lighting—daytime, a well-lit area, white walls, adding candles, lamps and spotlights will help.
2. Close all doors and windows and turn off any electrical appliances. You want as minimal noise interference as possible. If you live in the city or in a busy area, you may need to get up at three am to film. It'll be worth it.
3. Whilst outside may be romantic, seemingly serene and natural, it can be a pain in the rear for sound. Even the slightest breeze can interfere with the quality of the sound and nature and animals are pretty unpredictable.
4. The camera reduces your energy by ten to twenty per cent, so be over enthusiastic, rather than under. Smile at least twenty per cent more—trust me.
5. Be natural and be yourself. This means mistakes, mispronunciations and mumbles. Whilst practising your message is good, find a nice balance between "winging it" and over rehearsed. Your audience will notice the difference if you let it flow from the heart, rather than

from a script.

6. Cut out your "umms" and "ahhs" as much as you possibly can. This will interrupt the flow of your message.

7. Offer something via your video such as really practical information or instructions.

8. Use a tripod or put your device somewhere where it is stationery. A still video is a professional one.

9. Limit your background items.

10. If you're talking without having to demonstrate anything, just film from your shoulders up and zoom in quite close as it'll make it easier to connect if viewers can see your eyes.

11. Immediately make it clear what your product is or service offers, even if the video is not directly related.

12. Always guide your viewers over to your website and be sure to mention it at the start and end of the video. You can add text, so be sure to have your web address visibly prominent, either throughout the whole video or at the start and end.

13. Your video needs to have a very strong entertainment or informative component, rather than just advising people about your products or services, explain their background or history and add in some tips.

14. Keep your video under two minutes. People just don't have the attention span to stick with anything longer. The average length of the most viewed YouTube videos are between thirty to one hundred and twenty seconds.

15. Hook your audience's attention within the first ten seconds of your video or else you lose them to cat videos!

16. Connect to your viewers by using relatable and emotionally linking words, situations and content.

17. Once you have made it as short as possible, sleep on it and then make it shorter again.

18. Don't refer to your audience as 'guys' or 'youse'. Keep it tasteful and remember you are talking directly to one person.

19. Remember to keep your YouTube channel and videos

consistent with your branding. That means you need to use the same colours as your logo and website, add your logo wherever you can (a watermark looks the most professional or a banner in the background) and present yourself the way you want your business to be presented.

20. Ensure you make effective use of video tags. Use appropriate tag words that encapsulate your video and industry and will contribute to being more searchable.

21. Write a thorough description for your video in the section provided, inserting any keywords that you think people will search for.

Remember: being filmed dulls your energy levels, so I would exaggerate everything by twenty per cent more than what you would do in real life. For example, include more energy, enthusiasm, enunciation and vibrancy.

Video content ideas:
- how to make the perfect smoothie or favourite recipe
- yoga asana
- guided meditation
- introduce yourself
- post some beautiful images over the music you make
- display how you make jewellery, candles or artwork
- astrology reading
- psychic reading
- dance performance
- singing
- explain a technique that you've patented
- tutorial (for example, how to make a vision board)
- Q&A style
- cross promote with a fellow YouTuber!

Did you know? There are over 100 million hours of "how to" videos on YouTube.

Activity: Make a list of three to six of your favourite movies. You have my complete permission to take the day off and watch them all again if need be! For each movie, write down the first two words that bounce into your head that encapsulate these movies.

Then, next to each aspect below, write down one word that appeals to you most:

- visually
- words/sound/music
- feeling it left you with

Now write down elements of the story that remained with you, long after you finished watching it. Was there a gut wrenching twist? Did the story flow effortlessly? Were the characters so powerful in themselves that they drove the story? Once you have that written down, you have a blueprint for an entertaining video, which you can follow. As an intuitive and sensitive person, you will be able to tap into the energy of the emotion that you wish to express. Wrap yourself in that energy and project it through the camera as you are recording. It will have no choice but to affect the viewer whenever they watch it.

Remember: it's better to keep the video under two minutes. So your challenge will be to convey all this and distil it's essence down into a very short timeframe.

LinkedIn

As a professional in the holistic and wellbeing field, you may be quick to disregard LinkedIn, assuming that it's for those who work in the corporate world only. But the professional business networking site, which has been around for nearly twelve years, has over 300 million users3.6 million in Australia alone—and shouldn't be underestimated as a great marketing tool.

LinkedIn is important for a number of reasons. Not only is it an online resume, Facebook, forum and a recruitment database all rolled into one but your peers, clients and co-workers can endorse your skills and write recommendations for you.
It's also an easy way to let people know about your industry/work experience, knowledge and expertise. Rather than having to send people your complete resume, you can just share the URL to your LinkedIn profile with them this makes it much easier for sharing in other areas too, such as in your email signature, business card, other social media platforms and marketing collateral and so on.

Why is LinkedIn important for you?
1. It's a great way to share blog posts and articles that you have written (or have been written about you) much like you can on other social media platforms.
2. It's a great way for new people to discover you and your products or services.
3. It helps with your SEO and your general ability to be found on the internet.
4. It's another great way to promote yourself and your work digitally.
5. Sometimes LinkedIn networking groups can extend to real-life networking events, groups or clubs which can be a great opportunity to meet potential clients or have fun.
6. Other people share useful business links and resources.
7. You can also follow industry related companies and peers and see their updates.

How to maximise your profile:

1. Make sure you stand out from the crowd. The best way to do that is by highlighting your work let your skills; experience, awards and recognition do the talking for you.
2. Add references and recommendations between two and six is a good, readable number. Make sure they are specific and the person who has written the reference includes why they are recommending you and what project you worked on together.
3. Include an up to date professional headshot. "You're seven times more likely to have your profile viewed if you have one. Like a house that's on sale, the assumption is that if there's no photo, something's wrong." Forbes?
4. Ensure it is a hundred per cent up to date.
5. Keep your profile informative but succinct and readable. Long winded stories don't belong in your LinkedIn profile.
6. Ensure your contact details are current and accessible. A potential client will not bother if they cannot find your website, email or phone number easily.

What to avoid:

- a suggestive or sexy headshot. Just, no!
- too many updates that clog up people's newsfeeds
- the personal pictures of the baby/dog/renovation
- spamming anybody.

Remember: it's a professional networking site not a social networking site such as Facebook, so keep it completely professional.

Google+

Why join?

Google+ is a bit underrated in my opinion. It has the valuable
bonus of directly adding to your Google SEO because just like
YouTube, it's owned by Google (as the name suggests). It's a
more targeted social networking site with an aim to connect
people. You can imbed your YouTube clips straight into your
feed, so when people look at your profile, it's all there waiting
for them and they don't have to scroll through pages and pages.

Google+ has Google Hangouts which is this nifty little add on
where you can host webinars, live chats and video conferencing.
And hold onto your pants, because guess what? It's free.

The annoying thing is that you have to have a Gmail account,
which is not a terribly big deal but just another thing you have to
do. It's also another platform that you have to look after and can
be easy to neglect when you're new to it.

Websites

I could easily grant websites an ebook of their own; perhaps even a couple of volumes! But here's the least you should know about websites:

- I (and your customer) consider them vital
- you don't need to spend a fortune on one these days
- excellent copy is crucial. Copy means the writing that will be on your website.
- you can do it yourself BUT
- there are plenty of fantastic and talented website designers around. If you value your time and have some cash to invest in your social media marketing it is well worth the outlay.

Here's how you can help your website designer and ensure you get the best site.

- be upfront about your budget
- have your content, written and images, ready to go
- know exactly what you want on your site
- have a list of about three sites that you want your site to look and feel like
- have your logo and branding all ready to go.

What you'll need if you are going it alone:

- a registered domain name (there is a whole association in Australia dedicated to helping you with this: http://www.auda.org.au/)
- a website platform or CMS (content management system)
- content—written and images
- logo
- some time and patience
- the willingness to learn a new skill

'61% of SMEs with websites said this had improved the effectiveness of their business, mainly by increasing its exposure and facilitating information access for customers with 43% seeing increased customer awareness and 13%

Here are some places to go to create your own website:

- Wordpress.com or Wordpress.org
- Weebly.com
- Wix.com

They all offer a free basic package and then incrementally increase in subscription price depending on which add-ons and extras you want as part of your website.

Tip: you can check out your website's greatness by running it through this online analytical tool: www.marketing.grader.com

Domain names
How do I find out if a domain name is available?
http://whois.ausregistry.net.au/whois/whois_local.jsp

A domain extension is the small group of letters at the end of your URL. You may recognise these familiar ones:

- .com
- .com.au
- .net
- .biz
- .org
- .edu
- .gov

Originally, these suffixes had specific functions. They were:
.COM = commercial and was intended for commercial entities
.NET = network and was intended for organisations in network technologies
.ORG = organisation (for not-for-profit organisations)

These are considered "top level domain" name extensions and are important because they are more easily recognised and remembered and we feel safer with those extensions. Domain extensions that are less familiar might trigger our subconscious fear of spam and viruses. That being said, we're moving away from this line of thinking more and more, so it's not a hard and fast rule but if you want to err on the side of safety, try and catch yourself a dot com extension and avoid any hyphens or underscores in your domain name.

So we're in Australia. Should we au or not au? Research has shown that if someone searches for your website in Google, it is more likely to come up if you have .au at the end of your URL if they are doing an Australian specific search. My advice would be to grasp the dot com first but if that has already been secured by someone else then dot com dot au is the next best thing.

Did you know? You need an ABN (Australian Business Number) to register for .au at the end of your domain name.

Redirecting
It may also be worth considering registering several domain names that are similar to your chosen URL and redirect (or point) these to your website. WordPress has a function that can help you do this; otherwise seek out the help of a professional.

For example:
If your website is www.missymysterious.com, you might choose to register the following domains as well, providing they are available:
www.missymysterious.com.au
www.myssymysterious.com
www.mysteriousmissy.com

Keep in mind that this will cost you extra but might be worth it to capture any peripheral website traffic.

Remember: make sure your website is optimised for mobile devices as a high percentage of people now read websites this way. It's futile if you make it look fancy pants on your desktop and people are mostly reading it on their mobile devices.

Formula for headings (recommended):
    About the business
    About me
    Services/products
    Contact

Optional additions:
- Blog
- Events calendar
- Resources
- Online store/products/services
- Costs
- Useful links
- Testimonials
- Videos
- Media coverage
- Online courses

Tip: don't forget to include links to all your social media platforms in your contact section.

Content
After you've chosen your headings you now know what you have to write! Stick to one to two paragraphs per heading and sub heading if you can.

You may like to use this template below for your 'About Me' section.

About Me

My name is _____
I am a _____,
_____, _____
and _____.
The way I work
is_____
_____.
I value

_____

_____

.

My background is

_____

_____ .

I decide to make the switch to

_____ when

_____ [if applicable].

Did you know? [insert something very unique about yourself. For example, I competed in the Olympics]

My qualifications:

-

-

-

-

I have also studied:

-

-

-

-

I am a member of:

-

-

-

- [logos are ideal instead of listing]

Tip: for SEO purposes make sure the first and second sentence are SEO friendly. What do you want people to search for to find you? See the part about SEO in this ebook for more information.

Homepage
This is your website "foyer". It welcomes people and guides them to their next step. Waste no time in stating exactly what you do, services/products you offer, what your website is about

and what you can do for readers of your site.

The layout and content of this page is vital as most people will "land" on it. It needs to be easy to read, navigate, understand and have a clear "takeaway" message. For example, George is a massage therapist and school teacher based in Perth.

Keep your homepage very short but still cover the essentials. If someone only had time to view your homepage, will they know enough about your business?

Use a personal tone and tell people a story. Inform your readers straight away why you will help solve their problem. Don't be coy—be explicit. What sounds more effective to you?

Example A

This book will boost your sales and will make you known for doing what you love. It's an insightful guide on marketing for spiritually based businesses that is an easy and enjoyable read that will help you get your business or service noticed, quickly and inexpensively.

Example B

People have been saying for a while now that I should write an ebook and since I'm a writer I thought I should do that so here is a book on marketing. It started when I wrote about blogging but then I turned it into something more and now you get to read it.

Tip: keep your website consistent with your branding, style and voice.

Your products/services

Here is a template you can use to describe your product or service on your website.

This PRODUCT/SERVICE will do THIS ACTION for YOUR PROBLEM/CHALLENGE. IT IS THIS (list two to three features or benefits) and is for THESE PEOPLE THAT HAVE A NEED/PROBLEM and it is GOOD BECAUSE.

How important (out of ten) is it to write a decent product

description? Go on, have a guess! The answer is zero. Because you do not want to settle for decent, you want to aim for mind blowing and Earth shaking. The product description will be ultimately what sells your product, it'll be that final nail in the coffin that will either confirm to your users that they are a click away from living happily ever after or it will put them off and they'll run from the room and forget about what they were doing and never come back to purchase your product. My point: make it outstanding.

How to write good product copy.
Keep it brief. Have I said that much throughout this book?

Your product will be accompanied by an image (right? RIGHT?) but write the description as if the person cannot see the image.

Convey the most important features straight up, preferably in order of importance. Is it organic? Handmade? Are there only three in the world?

Next, communicate the benefits of using the product. For example, it will make you taller in two days and you will grow wings in your sleep. (If anyone actually sells this product, get in touch).

If there is anything negative about the product in the description, you're doing it wrong.

Tell me, directly, like you're talking to me face to face, what this product will do for me in as few words as possible.

Include specifics like measurements, weight, main ingredients etc in bullet points.

If you've done a little research on your product or have been selling it for a while, describe in one sentence what most buyers do with it or use it for. For example, these vials of blood make a great, quirky gift. Or these adult nappies team really well with the adult bibs. Double points if you link it back to one of your own products.

Tip: nearly 63 per cent of consumers indicate they are more likely to purchase from a site if it has product ratings and reviews. [http://www.searchenginejournal.com/the-power-of-social%C2%A0proof/21896/]

According to the website Visual.ly '…a good product review can hike up a product's sales by nine per cent, whilst a bad one can drag down someone's intention to buy by eleven per cent.' Although these are American statistics Australia often emulates these spending patterns and behaviours. http://visual.ly/us-social-commerce-%E2%80%93-statistics-and-trends

In 2013, Australians spent $37.1 billion via ecommerce and 53 per cent of people regularly buy from Australia. It is expected that 'international shoppers expected to spend $16 billion (AUD) annually with our local online retailers by 2018.' http://www.digitalbusiness.gov.au/2013/07/30/overseas-shoppers-spend-big-with-aussie-online-retailers-paypal-report/

Currently, the top two categories of goods purchased are: clothes, shoes and accessories ($12.5 billion) and health and beauty products ($7.6 billion). (same reference as above)

Content tips

Most will people spend less than a minute on your web page, so in order to grab their attention ensure you keep your copy snappy and engaging. Bullet points and short sentences work best. Don't waffle!

Keep your website copy professional. This means: no mistakes, minimise the colloquialisms and casual language and keep it informative rather than flowery. If in doubt, hire a copywriter to do this for you—another sound investment in your marketing practises.

Aim to keep your "About" page to less than three hundred words and keep each event, service or product that you list to one hundred words. Most other pages (such as "Contact") should only include an introductory sentence or two.

Include a "call to action" on as many pages as possible. A call to action is a direction given to your readers to make them do something, for example 'book today', 'contact me now', and 'buy this product immediately'. One call to action per page is more than enough.

Make life easy for your website viewer. Everything needs to be obvious and labelled—don't make them hunt around for things or they will give up and go elsewhere.

Write your complete website copy and then put it away for a week (at the very least). Relook at it with fresh eyes and edit it ruthlessly. Reduce the word count by at least ten per cent.

Brevity: this is vital. Don't over explain and cut it down.

Most people scan rather than read each page in detail, so include keywords that will pick up people's attention (this will also help with SEO). Keep descriptive and flowery language for your poetry—there's no place for words like 'amazing, wonderful, magnificent' etc in your website copy (testimonials are a different matter).

Incorporate:
- bullet points
- the inverted pyramid method (see the chapter on blogging)
- hyperlinks to internal webpages or external webpages that are relevant
- one idea per paragraph
- no clichés
- meticulous proofreading

- headings, paragraphs, highlighting and dot points.

Avoid too much repetition. If you've said something twice, that's enough.

Your content has to do something—provide something, ask something, offer something, encourage the reader to DO something. For example, 'call me today' or 'here are some facts on back pain'.

Hook your readers in with inviting questions or statements. 'Want to be more creative?' Boom, you have their attention. The hook should be a succinct summary of what you offer and the benefits of. It'll make readers think, 'yes, I NEED that. That's why I'm here'.

Create a connection with the reader. Write your copy as if you are addressing one person directly, rather than a group. For example, 'I will do this for YOU.'

Be direct, clear and decisive in your wording. "Maybe", "perhaps" and other non-committal words should not feature in your static website copy. Static pages are the ones that have longevity as opposed to your blog which is constantly updated.

Online courses

One of the best things about the internet is its ability to reach people that you may not be able to reach in real life. People with mobility issues or from a different geographical space can enjoy the benefits of the products or services you offer.

If you teach workshops or courses, why not offer it as an online option? You can add a widget or a learning management system to your website that will help you deliver these online courses, all you have to do is write the content. Most online course plugins can be used with WordPress and can even handle the money side of things. It's worth doing some research to find a plugin that has the features that you want to incorporate into your course.

Here are some to look at:
- http://member.wishlistproducts.com/
- Coursepress
- LearnPress

Google Analytics

Who looks at your website?

Most blogging platforms will have an inbuilt statistical analysis program to show you an overview of how many people are looking at your blog. It's an excellent way to get an idea of what is appealing to your audience and what they're reading.

Google has its own analytics program which you can use for free and provides a much more accurate count and even breaks the analysis down into categories such as geographical location, age, time spent on your site and other variables and you can compare over any time period. It can even tell you which pages of your website are converting your viewers in active purchasers. Perhaps that blog post you wrote last month has pushed through some additional sales?

A helpful part of Google Analytics is to see where people are referred from. It might say 60 per cent come from Facebook or from a peer's website. You can see what works in terms of promoting your site and where to maintain your efforts.

SEO

This will be a simple overview in SEO. You may want to look at investing in some quality resource materials about the best way to optimise your site and online tools or do your own further research.

SEO stands for search engine optimisation. This is the process of optimising how discoverable you are on the internet and making your web content easily searchable, therefore increasing the traffic to your site. You know when you type in a search term and the search engine comes up with literally hundreds of thousands of pages? How many pages do you actually scroll through? Most only take notice of the first three links; maybe if you have the time, you'll scroll through two or three pages. The better you have optimised your website, the more likely it will show up higher (closer to the top of the list) in the search rankings.

How do you optimise your website for search engines?
The easiest strategy is to have a look at your words—do they match searchable content? My website is Incense and Happiness, so I made sure I could slip in those words and other relevant key terms as much as possible without making the content sounding naff. But make sure you don't overdo it—search engines will recognise this and will not rank your site. It's quite the precarious balance!

Google has an algorithm that it uses to rank pages. Understanding the exact mechanics of the algorithm is for the aficionados. But there are some general guiding principles that you can work with to ensure that you're in the game. The updated algorithm places more of an emphasis on quality of the site, rather than quantity. This means it's more important to have relevant and useful content on your site rather than a lot of "spammy" sites linking to yours.

Keywords

Keywords are a major ally in boosting your SEO. What words will people search with to find you in the chaos that is the internet? These are the words that you will use that sum up what your website is all about. It's a good idea to create a list of these words. Refer back to your original list that you used to create your mission statement.

Here are some guidelines
Having a blog helps particularly if it is part of your website. Ranking is affected by how recent the content is and with a blog you are updating your content frequently.

Make sure you update your other website content regularly and that it is current.

When writing your blog posts, make sure some or most of them are targeted towards a broader demographic and have longevity. But don't sacrifice good quality writing.

Google favours those sites that use their paid advertising feature called Google Adwords.

Use other social media platforms to send people to your website. The more people that look at your website; the more that search engines recognise that it's a well trafficked site and thus rank you higher

If you are a location based service, rather than just existing online, make sure you use your city and/or state as one of your most prominent keywords. This will help when people are searching. For example, someone may type "robes Hobart" to search for a robe in Hobart. If you sell robes and are located in Hobart or online, you should definitely utilise these keywords.

Make sure you have two or three target keywords for each webpage, not just the website as a whole.

Google now prefers longer articles of approximate one thousand words. This is where you have to decide whether you'd rather have more hits, or keep your readers interested. If you can craft an interesting, informative and entertaining post of one thousand words, go for it! But be warned, this can be challenging, especially if you're not a professional writer. Likewise, make sure your content is unique. Don't bother with generic or stolen content (also known as spun content) and keep your content information rich. Write for the visitor, not for the search engines.

The Google algorithm (at the time of publication) values real audience interaction. If it can tell that people are visiting and engaging with your site regularly, it will view it favourably when knowing where to place it in search rankings. It's important to have an easy way for your audience to interact with your site. This could be via a comments section, product reviews, voting polls etc. Most website platforms have these widget options readily available.

Make sure when you upload your images, you are including keywords in their titles as well as their "alt titles". If you are using WordPress you'll have both of these fields to fill in when you upload your images. The word must pertain to the image; otherwise you are in violation of Google's policy. If you violate too many of Google's rules you are at risk of being penalised by having poor rankings and nobody wants that!

Sign up and use Google Webmaster Tools as this will help you be more searchable via Google (the biggest search engine in the world). The instructions are quite comprehensive and may look daunting and intimidating and full of computer jargon. Experiment and break it down a step at a time and you will be surprised at what you achieve.

Make sure your site is easy to navigate. People should be able to find what they need with less than two or three clicks.

Websites rank higher with YouTube videos imbedded because Google owns YouTube.

Make your domain name easily searchable and pertaining to your business.

Get other sites to link back to your site. The more genuine

websites that link to your own site the more Google trusts your site to be worthwhile; however it's more important to be linked from another site that is a quality site rather than many sites of lesser quality.

Remember: you can always hire a SEO expert to help you and they are well worth their money. Make sure you find a reputable one with plenty of references or testimonials.

Did you know? Any books or resources (such as courses or fact sheets etc) about this topic should be published or revised after 2014 because Google has changed its policies many times—what worked in 2012 may now get you banned.

Helpful links:
Search Engine Journal:
http://www.searchenginejournal.com
To keep up to speed on Google's search ranking policies, read here:
www.support.google.com/webmasters/bin/answer.py?w=en&answer=35769rules
Check if your domain name has ever been registered before and if it has been blacklisted
Web.archive.org:
To find any broken links on your site:
www.home.snafu.de/tilman/xenulink.html
Insert two more links here

Useful programs

Here are some lists of software or platform recommendations to try. They vary from being geared for beginners to experts and offer a variety of functions – all with the aim of making your life and business administration easier.

CRM/sales:
- Salesforce
- Jobber
- Webmerge
- PlanPlus Online
- Zencash
- Lending Core
- Megaventory
- Acuity
- Atlassin
- Namaste Lite
- Infusionsoft
- MindBody

Other social media platforms to explore:
Reddit
Quora
Flickr
Ning
Yelp
LinkedIn
Pinterest
Slideshare
StumbleUpon

There are also things called listening tools. These are social media tools to help pick up what is being talked about through social media. You can refine the search criteria using key words which could comprise of your company name, industry or products. It's a great way to gauge what is being said about you on the internet (particularly if you are a larger business) or find out trends in the industry and is a quick way to find out what discussion is happening that you can contribute to. Most of these applications work on a free model with an option to upgrade at a cost which includes more features and benefits.

Some listening tools include:
Social Mention
Mention
Twazzup (Twitter only)
Addict-o-Matic
How Sociable
Ice Rocket

It's also worth signing up to Google Alerts, which will send you an email with the specified search terms (use your name and business name, include your city) if it commonly comes up in Google searches. This is handy in case someone has mentioned you on their website or blog that you weren't aware of.

Extra handy things:
PlaceIt
ShortStack—great for running social media competitions plus their blog is a treasure chest of information
Storify—a handy tool to collect all your tweets about a particularly hashtag or topic
Haiku Deck—a presentation application to display slides. It's like a fancy, more "now" version of PowerPoint.
http://750words.com/ - a writing inspirational tool

Organising your social media content:
Here is a handy diagram of where you can flood your content (that's your blog posts, video, website content etc) out into the wider areas of the internet. Remember to work on the fundamentals first before you even bother with most of these things. This should be in your six to twelve month plan, or even later.

Traffic Mindmap:
http://www.buzzblogger.com/wp-

content/uploads/2014/01/trafficmindmap.pdf

Twellow
Helps you search Twitter via groups and industries.
http://www.twellow.com/

Shortstack
This is a useful website that heaps and heaps of handy hints
about all social media platforms in an easy to read way.

These are particularly useful if you have a product or service that
can be sold internationally:
Video:
Veoh
Vimeo
WonderHowTo
Ustream

Customers and sales

Without your clients or customers you wouldn't be able to do what you love and get paid for it, so let's explore a few ways that we can increase customer loyalty and sales to ensure that you are able to continue to expand your business in a way that is right for you, whilst continuing to help your beloved customers.

The Pareto Principle

The Pareto Principle is a strategic mathematic philosophy used in marketing that claims that 80 per cent of your sales come from twenty per cent of your clientele.
This means you need to:
- nourish your existing clients
- reward your clients
- offer clients support
- genuinely praise your clients
- hold them in the highest esteem and don't criticise them behind their back.

So if it's revenue you are after, it's time to focus on your bestselling products and services (that twenty per cent of your business that brings in most of your income) and spend less time on the other eighty per cent of your products/services or leave these completely up to another soul. I can assume that there are other factors to running your business than just financial reward, so this may not necessarily apply to you but there is no shame in making a profit.

The distribution is claimed to appear in several different aspects relevant to businesses. For example:
- 80 per cent of a company's profits come from 20 per cent of its customers
- 80 per cent of a company's complaints come from 20 per cent of its customers
- 80 per cent of a company's sales are made by 20 per cent of its sales staff
- 80 per cent of a company's profits come from 20 per cent

of the time its staff spend

• 80 per cent of a company's sales come from 20 per cent of its products

If there's one thing that you need to consistently remember when marketing, it's that people are fundamentally narcissistic. Remember this and you'll always be on the right track when marketing things. Always remember that you are telling potential and current clients how they will be affected by your service, what you can do for them! It's not about you, it's always about them. Everything is about them when you are engaging in marketing. The words you choose; the images you choose.

We've established that it's much cheaper to keep existing customers than to find new ones, which is why it's always valuable to consider a loyalty scheme or system (don't be put off by the word scheme).

There are many companies that specialise in loyalty programs that you may wish to look into to find a system that works for you and that isn't too time consuming.

Here are a number of ideas you can use as a loyalty program:
- reward loyal customers with ad hoc specials and discounts (you can use a discount code or just offer them privately if you have a small customer base)
- use an old fashioned stamp card system, much like some coffee shops still use, and reward multiple purchases
- Use a VIP system where customers can either pay a nominal amount or after they have spent a certain amount with you they become part of the VIP program which can offer them various benefits, such as discounts, exclusive events/information or special offers.
- Points system: each dollar can be a point and they can accumulate certain points to spend on products/services that you stipulate.
- Digital loyalty card program, there are many of these available now and can offer a range of benefits and retention options for your customers.
- Around special events (Christmas, clients' birthdays or your business's birthday works well) offer a discount voucher or gift card to your loyal clients. Explain they are receiving it because of their loyalty and that it means a lot to you that they continue to use your services.
- Friend referral incentives—for every friend they refer who books an appointment or purchases a product, you offer a discount on the referee's next purchase.
- special access to prizes and competition draws

- Team up with another company/business to offer incentives to your loyal customers that they can provide. This is also a great way of cross promoting both businesses, if you return the service in kind.

If you have a sign up process that accompanies your loyalty program, it can also be a really great way of collecting data that you can use in your promotional activities. Remember to capture their contact details and other relevant information (see the section on target demographics).

Did you know? Eighty four per cent of consumers would switch brands for prize incentives and 80 per cent buy more from companies of whom they are members, according to Edge Loyalty.

Upselling

Upselling is a way of increasing your revenue without having to convince a new demographic to purchase what you do.

Think about ways in which you can value add to your existing primary demographic/existing clients. This is not about putting the hard sell and squeezing more money out of them, this is about offering them choices and extra pathways if they wish to deepen their experience with you.

Make sure you communicate with them that there are extra avenues you offer, don't assume just because they are a client that they know everything you offer. Communicate that you have product to offer them that will help after a healing session perhaps, or that you have purchasable downloadable meditations on your website or that you are holding a workshop on something they would be interested in soon.

Upselling can transcend from verbal communication into your marketing as well. For example, if you are sending a confirmation email to someone attending a workshop or thanking them for recently using your service, you could include a sentence asking 'have you considered this product/service' (include hyperlinks of course!)

Tip: reward your customers with a discount on any additional product or service.

Product promotional strategy

As you are beginning to learn, promotion and marketing is an ongoing venture. It's not something that can be done once and results will flood in. Here's an example strategy that you could use to plan out a promotional strategy for one product for your digital marketing (create one for all your products, events and services). You may also like to create a similar one for traditional marketing techniques such as a PR campaign, launch event and so forth.

Timeframe	Strategy	Activities
Two to four weeks prior to release date.	Pre-announcement	'Guess what's coming?' Announce timeframe and offer an opportunity for backorders. Even if the product is not entirely ready, this is a good technique to gain momentum.
Day of product release.	Release	Offer a special discount, bonus or two for one offer. Make it a celebration; perhaps have a physical or online launch. It's also a great opportunity for a competition, giveaways and other activities that generate hype. This activity can span over several days.
One to six weeks after release.	Response to release	After the product has been released, capture the excitement and response (always promote only the positive), testimonials, impressive sales figures, feedback, joy it has brought you and anecdotes all work well. Share photos of your

		clients/customers using or buying your product, particularly if it is tangible.
This should be an ongoing activity whilst the product is available.	Slow drip reminders	You can use snippets of the above activities spread out sporadically. Provide insights as to how to use the product, it's back story, how people have responded to the product and how they incorporate it into their daily lives. Remember to share any media coverage that you receive don't be shy!
Six to twelve months after the release.	Push sale/offer	Competition, sales, discount, special offers. This should be coinciding with advertising, public relations and contacting bloggers to review your product. Your friends, family and networks should all be familiar with your product/s or services by now.
Twelve months after the release	Anniversary	Celebrate the anniversary since the product's release with giveaways and use the opportunity to promote any upcoming or new products.

Remember: each product should sell the next product in some way.

Soft Launch
Rather than creating a lot of buzz around releasing a new product you could try having a soft launch for your product or blog and then start promoting it in four to six months time. This creates a

sense of FOMO (fear of missing out) in people and a thought process of 'why didn't I know about this? I will now actively stay in touch to ensure I never miss anything from this person again'. Back to that social proof thing again!

FAQ

Here, I've addressed some common and frequent questions that I get asked.

Do I have to use social media?

No you don't. Plenty of businesses run successfully without using it at all. However, I would suggest that since you have picked up this book that your higher self is guiding you towards considering how it will help you. And if you don't use it to promote your business, your competitors are going to be one step ahead of you.

Should I hire someone or do it myself?

This is up to you. If you really detest it, it may be worth bringing in someone to help. Let's face it; life is short, so let's spend it doing what we love. And just as you are an expert in what you do, marketing people are experts in what they do. It is worth being aware of what you are and aren't willing to do to really promote your business without running yourself to the ground. Hopefully, by reading this book it has made this decision clearer for you.

Should I stop swearing?

I encourage authenticity and genuineness wherever possible. If you use swear words and think that is part of who you are, I can't see why you should be conservative in your social media efforts.

You may choose to keep your personal Facebook and business pages separate—perhaps the business page is a little softer or consistent in its tone and you choose to use more formal language. If you've ever pondered whether you should cut down your swearing or become more conservative, again this may be Spirit pushing you in that direction.

What is traffic?

Traffic means the influx of people (or "bots" in some cases) that are looking at your website or online content (your videos, blogs etc). Traffic can be direct, referral or search engine (organic and paid). Direct traffic is those people that put your URL straight into the browser bar. They know exactly what they're looking for and head to your stuff straight away. These people are key because they already know who you are, what you do and they are likely going to be your biggest buyers.

Referral traffic are people that come from other sites. When people link to your website in their blog posts, blog roll, website or just general promotion they are referring traffic to your site (assuming people click on it). Although it can be hard to find a network of people that are willing to do this, there is a sure fire way you can increase your chances—have outstanding content! People are more likely to link to you if you have something of value to offer and excellent information to be shared. Ensure your social networks are strong because most referral traffic comes from social media. Offer people incentives to link to your site, such as a discount on their next product, a commission or create an affiliate marketing program for them (you might need to do a bit more research into affiliate marketing before you get started).

Search engine traffic are the people that come to you via search engines such as Google etc. Most of this traffic will be searching a keyword or phrase before they discover your site. 'Organic' results are the people that just search and find your content and 'paid' is when you pay Google or other search engines to list you in a prominent position amongst the search results. You can do this via Google Adwords which will show your tailored advert in the right hand column or in a banner above the organic search results.

How can I go viral?
"Going viral" is a buzzword marketing technique that means a focal point of your marketing campaign spreads like a computer virus. Remember that short video of a baby being fitted with new glasses for the first time that spread across Facebook like wildfire during early 2015? That is an example of content "going viral".

In short, the answer is no. I would question your motivations to go viral. Sure, the instant world or nationwide fame may be thrilling but in a few days you will be forgotten. Good marketing is a consistent and regular effort— much like a friendship or relationship. "Going viral" is analogous to a passionate one night stand.

There's also a real element of luck to "going viral" and if you are still convinced that it is important to you and your business, I would encourage that you have a solid digital marketing strategy and website in place first to take advantage of the increased reach.

Should I purchase advertising?
Paid advertising to draw customers or draw customers to make money to pay advertising? That is the age old chicken or egg question. You'll know the right decision for you. What sits right within you? If you don't know yet, you can always put off advertising (if your services/products are not time sensitive) for a month or two to decide and feel comfortable with your decision.

My view is that booking advertising puts a message out to the Universe. It says, 'here! I have this product or service I believe in and you should too'. Make sure you are ready for the positive repercussions of advertising. Ensure your business is fully established, products and services are tested and ready. Otherwise you may have to turn away or disappoint clients or customers, damaging your brand or business's reputation.

What about copyright?
At the time of writing this book Copyright in Australia is undergoing a reform and the current copyright legislation states that you cannot use anyone else's material without their permission and/or acknowledgment. This includes images (even those ripped off the internet), writing, music, blog posts, artwork and videos etc. You are NOT breaching copyright if you: click the share button on your Facebook page and share someone's original material (as Facebook attributes it back to the poster).

Vanessa Jones is an author and writer from Adelaide, South Australia. She's also the Marketing Manager for SA Writers Centre, a copywriter, freelance marketing consultant and yoga instructor. Vanessa holds an Advanced Diploma of Professional Writing and has won awards for her poetry and short stories and has been published in *The Hoopla, Lip Magazine, Southern Write* and *Independent Weekly*.